Sustainability in Pet Care

Lessons in Leadership, Innovation, and
Sustainability from the Frontlines of Pet Care

Alex McKinnon

For information, contact:
Alex McKinnon
Charlotte, NC
damckinnon@aol.com

Learn more at: www.sustainabilityinpetcare.com.

ISBN: 979-8-9999814-0-0

Printed in the United States of America
First Edition

Cover design by Bridget Mills of www.creative-vortex.com

Dedication

Very importantly, I would like to thank many who have been so helpful in helping me to write this book. While the list is incomplete at best, here are some of them.

To my wife DeDe and our rescue dogs Skye and Erin, thank you for your support in countless ways.

To my colleagues at Kinn including Jason Spooner, Bridget Soden Mills, Candace Gasper, and Amber Smith Dash. A big thank you to so many expert pet pros across the country who jumped at the opportunity to help us by sharing your insights and wisdom.

This includes thank yous for the amazing interviews provided by Charlotte Biggs (decades of experience in pet care as business owner, consultant, COO of IBPSA, etc.), Mark Klaiman (Founder and Co-Owner of Pet Camp in San Francisco), Dr. Josh Fisher (Director of Animal Care & Control in Charlotte), Jennifer Wolf-Pierson (Leader of ABC Pet Resort, Pet Care Boot Camp, Thought Leader, and Speaker), Ben Day (decades of safety experience in pet care and former COO of IBPSA), Jerrica Owen (Executive Director of National Animal Care and Control Association), Jess Okon (decades of experience in grooming, running boarding facilities, training, etc., including sales at Blue-9), Dom Hodgson (global pet consultant and coach with European and North American expertise over the past few decades), Alex Varney (8 years of operational experience running Pinnacle Pet in Ohio), Anna Radel (21 years of experience including owning/running Fieldstone Animal Inn, Coach/consultant for the Dog Gurus), Dianna Starr (owner of Cleanwise with decades of animal care experience), Scott Learned (decades of experience designing facilities for animal shelters and boarding facilities), Brad Shear (30 years of experience operating animal shelters and CEO Potter League of Animals), Matt Pepper (decades of animal shelter leadership experience and CEO Michigan Humane), Apryl Steele (30 years of experience including 20 years as Veterinarian and over a decade leading Humane Colorado as CEO), Dan Poirier (13 years of experience including being co-founder and co-owner of both 2 locations of Fetch & Catch facilities in Buffalo and co-founder and co-owner of PACKPRO), Eve Molzhon (12 years of experience in pet care as Owner of several businesses including Dog Handler Academy), and Gary Weitzman (decades of experience as Veterinarian and President San Diego Humane Society).

Table of Contents

"In a growth mindset, challenges are exciting rather than threatening. So rather than thinking, oh, I'm going to reveal my weaknesses, you say, wow, here's a chance to grow."
— *Carol S. Dweck, Ph.D.*, author of *Mindset: The New Psychology of Success*

Introduction

Are you looking for ways to improve sustainability in your pet or animal care facility? This book is written exactly for that purpose, and is designed for leaders at pet boarding facilities and/or animal shelters.

I've organized the book by focusing on stories and case studies from leading experts in the animal shelter and pet boarding industries that teach you WHY and HOW to sustainably solve problems for better outcomes with animals, staff, the environment, and time/cost, or as we call them, the 4 P's Pets, People, Planet, and Profit.

While professionals at boarding facilities and animal shelters do use different "languages," e.g. animals vs. pets or progress vs. profit, we hope you will stick with us, as we think we all have a lot to learn from one another.

We are going to start off by defining the scope of the book in a few ways. First, the concept of sustainability is not just about the environment, but also encompasses better outcomes for animals, people, the planet, and cost savings/money.

Why?

If you want to become world class at your boarding facility or animal shelter, you have to excel in all 4 of these areas, or you won't be around to tell about it.

Why did we include in the scope both pet boarding and animal shelters? Each of these areas, despite their differences, have much in common with each other. Importantly, they both have huge impacts on their segments of pet care. Boarding is the largest business segment for pet resorts in the USA. Animal shelters, as most of you know, literally are the difference between life and death for far too many dogs and cats in North America.

Also, both of these areas involve the most contact time with animals, as they include animal overnight lodging. So by taking an overview of these two segments, we hope to help people in both areas to learn best practices from one another, especially since the time animals spend at these types of facilities are amongst the longest within the pet care industry.

We believe that most readers will find multiple, totally new ideas in this book to improve sustainability, including some that seem to come from out of left field. One of those new and different sources for you could be related to the fact that Alex also co-founded a Pet Ministry at Covenant Presbyterian Church in Charlotte, NC, where the links to sustainability in pet care are already significant and growing rapidly.

To be clear, this book is NOT about being Presbyterian, these ideas could work for most types of spirituality. Based on what the Pet Ministry team have done in their first 3 years, he has seen it influence sustainability improvements with animals, staff, the environment, and their financials across animal shelters and pet boarding facilities, not to mention veterinarians. We will cover these in the coming chapters.

Another topic that is important to lead off with in the introduction is mindset. If you have not ever read the book Mindset by Carol S. Dweck, I give it my highest rating. She educates the reader on the differences between a Fixed Mindset and a Growth Mindset.

As far as this book goes, you are going to get much more out of it if you have a Growth Mindset while reading the book and implementing lessons learned. In other words, this book is not written for those who believe they already know everything about running their pet business.

Yes, unfortunately there are plenty of people like that out there. Think about examples of some businesses started 20-30 years ago as a kennel offering overnight boarding, and remain that same way today. Compare that to a "pet resort" that has evolved over the years from Boarding, to adding DayCare, then training, and finally grooming, and has developed an "enrichment" mindset. The latter type of business is much more likely to be open to improving their sustainability.

Enrichment is a theme related to sustainability that spans boarding facilities and other pet resort businesses where it has been around for years. However, enrichment has recently become a growing force in animal shelters as well. As such, we will often touch on this important and growing trend in pet care.

"Sustainability is creating long-term solutions for animals, people, and the environment."
— *Jerrica Owen*, Executive Director, National Animal Care & Control Association

Chapter 1: Understanding Sustainability in Pet Care

How do you define sustainability in the context of pet/animal care?

Some people say the environment. Others emphasize pet health and wellness. Yet many others say it is people, because all service businesses are people driven. Then again, the government and others say it is about money. After having been in the industry for over 12 years, I would say it is all of these. Or as we say in the for-profit world, the 4 P's Pets, People, Planet, and Profits, which for the animal shelters is often classified as animals, people, environment, and cost savings.

One of the best simple definitions I have heard came from Jerrica Owen, Executive Director of the National Animal Care and Control Association, when she said sustainability involves "long-term solutions." A related and important comment from Charlotte Biggs is that "sustainability is a movement."

Although there are many differences between pet boarding facilities and animal shelters, there are many more similarities that most people realize. Each of them focuses on the long-term health and wellness of animals. All have staffing issues. They share many environmental challenges both at the design and operational levels. Whether they are for-profit or non-profit, many businesses continue to struggle today with a lack of resources and need more ways to save money.

Another way to look at the similarities between all pet businesses is that many of them are struggling with the costs, including start-up costs and especially implementation. Also, there are ongoing issues related to education of staff. Importantly, pet businesses of all types continue to suffer from problems related to a lack of Standard Operating Procedures, aka SOPs.

This is not only related to whether they have effective SOPs, but also to issues when the staff question the SOPs. This requires much more education on WHY the procedures are needed, and why the best ones are the most suitable ones for the business.

In particular, staff need to be educated not only to focus on the outcomes with animals, people, the environment, and costs, but also to ensure that the processes constantly monitor the business' TIME, TALENT, and TREASURE.

"The health and safety of animals has got to be priority number one for a sustainable pet care business."
— *Mark Klaiman*, Founder and Co-Owner of Pet Camp (San Francisco)

Chapter 2: Prioritizing Better Outcomes for Animals

If you take a poll of what is the most important aspect of sustainability in pet care across boarding facilities and animal shelters, while there may be some differences, without a doubt prioritizing better outcomes for animals is usually at the top of the list.

In other words, between improving outcomes for animals, staff, the environment, and money, ensuring the health and welfare of animals through sustainable practices is usually priority number one.

Improving animal welfare through facility design and supplies:

Ideally, a good place to start in the area of prioritizing better outcomes with animals would be with the design of the facility, as these decisions will be made up front, and have a lifetime impact on animals. Charlotte Biggs who owned a pet boarding facility in Texas for 15 years, was a pioneer in sustainable design of pet facilities. Way ahead of the curve, here are some of Charlotte's original ideas focused on sustainability, and especially for pets' better health:

- Building placement so that the right areas of the building are facing the sun at the right times of day to optimize the pet's experience, health and comfort.

- Having an aerobic septic system for improved water quality, reduced environmental impact, and better water conservation. The facility was in Texas and as her only source of water, she had a rainwater collection system.

- Installing an HVAC system designed to optimize air turnover to minimize animal health issues.

When running her own pet resort facility in south Florida, Jess Okon had some great learnings in terms of becoming more sustainable with cleaning supplies, which included cleaning chemicals, shampoo, conditioner, etc.

A not infrequent issue was that employees used these concentrated cleaning supplies straight out of the bottle without any dilution.

This resulted in waste of chemicals and overly harsh application when the chemicals were not diluted to the properly designed and balanced strength. She got her team to set up metered dispensing systems that automatically inserted the right amount of water into the cleaning supplies to bring them to the desired concentrations. The automated metered system delivered many sustainability benefits including saving time which can be reallocated to more enrichment for happier, more enriched pets.

This also empowered employees to make a container of cleaning supplies to go from lasting 1 week to 3+ weeks, all by simply using the products the way they were properly designed to be used.

Eve Molzhon shares a great story, and the author has heard very similar versions of this on so many occasions, in terms of how to significantly improve the outcomes for dog health by asking questions and testing processes, until you get the right approach. In other words, learn from how NOT to do something.

She was speaking with the owner of a kennel who had many cage banks in a boarding room, all utilizing a drain in the middle of the floor. The owner explained that to clean they used a hose, spraying to move things along and also used lots of chemicals.

That meant that all the pee, dirt, grime, and feces were being sprayed first onto the back wall, then the side walls, etc. in order to move all the bad stuff into the middle of the room where the drain was. In other words, when they sprayed, the bad stuff went everywhere, even though there were live animals in the room, who were actually getting sprayed with some of the bad stuff.

When Eve asked the owner about the impact on animals, she said she had never thought about that. Eve suggested that she do a test using the hose, and children's finger paint, so that she could see where the spraying made the finger paint land. When Eve spoke with this owner a few months later, she heard the owner confess that the finger paint test opened her eyes to the fact that a lot of bad stuff was ending up on the dogs nearby.

Eve asked her many more questions, which also led to her admit that there was no code and thus no process for ever cleaning out the drain in the middle of the room, so all the bad stuff was either stuck in there for many months, and/or they had to use lots of powerful chemicals to occasionally try to disguise the smell and/or clean it up.

When talking about how to provide better outcomes for pets, be certain to include how to be sure you can effectively and efficiently sanitize the space. Eve also shared some good ideas with us involving enrichment. One idea is to have enrichment happen in a large suite so the dog can go in and do their thing without human intervention, in other words, the dogs are making their own fun.

You can either build a suite in a hallway or in an outside play area and house the enrichment there. This can also work very well for dogs who are not in group play, but rather part of a private play program. Some of the options for sanitizing this space that she recommends include a blue light wand, a laser wand, and/or a static spray machine instead of spraying chemicals. She emphasizes that these spaces could use a lot of easier to clean materials, and/or use fabric snuffle mats which you can put in the laundry to clean along with rags and towels. In addition, vinegar-based cleaning can be a great way to clean without many harsh chemicals in areas where it is effective.

That the health and safety of animals must be priority #1 for a sustainable business is the author's perspective, and Mark Klaiman agrees. He also agrees that there is a lot of sustainability crossover between solutions to produce better outcomes for animals, staff, planet, and money. A great place to start is with chemicals, with a focus on usage, reducing use, and/or using better chemicals.

He has seen improvements with dogs, better use of the staff's time, and a positive environmental impact when that area becomes a focus. He also talks a lot about his facility's change from using foaming guns to electrostatic sprayers.   This created many benefits including better cleaning efficiency, in especially hard-to-reach areas. Other benefits included using fewer chemicals, water, and power resulting in a healthier outcome for dogs and cats.

Mark also believes that there is a lot of shared ground between sustainability and enrichment. As an example, about a year ago Mark opened a new pet resort location called Ranger Station. It was designed from the ground up to be "organic." There are real rocks, the bridge is made of real wood, and there are "wild spaces" truly unique in its urban location. There is also a sensory garden made of plants. As you can imagine, dogs love this place for so many reasons.

Dianna's experience in wet/dry cleaning systems has shown time and again that getting your pet facility really clean has a direct link to the health and welfare of not only pets, but staff as well. She has had countless clients with old school thoughts on cleaning processes who have insisted on using bleach and mops as they say they have always had good results with these but nonetheless were experiencing ongoing outbreaks of illnesses with pets.

They argued that both bleach and mops were cheap and were good enough. However, when she has been successful in getting pet facilities to drop the bleach and mops and go to more modern wet/dry cleaning systems the outbreaks stopped, and did not return.

Dianna also recommends that facilities work with more progressive architects on building design, speak with others in the industry in the region in which you are opening, and work with proven pros in the pet industry design space to avoid the mistakes that others have experienced whether they are non-profit or for profit.

Scott Learned's team doing design work for facilities takes a long view on what is best for the animal's outcomes. This can allow for savings in some areas to be repurposed for even better dog welfare through enrichment activities and healthier surroundings.

Apryl also points out that dogs want choice. While this most often is difficult in a kennel, her team has a special way of making their dogs calmer and happier by providing them with some important choice options in their kennels. The kennel front sides are half frosted and half clear, which lets the dogs decide if they want to be more or less seen.

This lets them be introverted at some times, and more extroverted at others, which the dogs love. Another important benefit of choice they offer the dogs with their kennels is that one half of the floor is heated, and the other half not heated. This lets the dogs decide if they want to be warmer or cooler, or to switch back and forth. This is also complemented by Apryl's team by having natural lighting let into all dog kennels to help them sense day and night cycles.

For some areas, another sustainable option as a water source could be what the author encountered on a recent trip to South Africa where there was no option of getting water from a local municipality, and rainwater collecting systems could be sporadic, and not helpful during dryer times of the year.

When an area offers these features, an innovative source of clean water for animals demonstrated in South Africa included the excavation of a well to access clean water year-round, with the added feature of a small solar panel right next to it. This allows the use of power generated by the solar panel installation to reliably bring well water to the surface. In those areas the residents pump the water into a drinking pool for the animals – a true win-win-win situation.

Enrichment and training as a way to improve pets' wellbeing:

Dom's view on improving outcomes for pets is all about enrichment. The staff of many of his coaching clients start off offering unlimited play all day long which results in the dogs suffering from overstimulation, exhaustion, high stress, behavioral issues, and even fights. He has seen many positive turnarounds when switching from free play to enrichment, focusing on small group activities, personalized activities, and good-better-best offerings, while charging a premium.

Across the board, he sees happier dogs and happier clients. This also saves the businesses time by switching from free play to set activity times, very often with scent room activities followed by scheduled rest for the dogs. If you are not familiar with scent rooms, here is some more information on what they are and why they work.

As a dog's superpower is their sense of smell, it only takes a small room to set up with different scents for the dog to sniff. Dom notes that some research indicates that ten minutes of sniffing scent can be the equivalent of 40 minutes of walking. So, scent rooms are great to calm energy levels and to increase confidence, both of which may be a good precursor to placing a dog into a group.

Alex Varney's expertise in achieving better outcomes for pets encompasses a strategy which balances socialization with personalization, depending on the animal. She understands that many dogs are not that social, so her team personalizes the programs with different socialization options as enrichment add-ons. Some of these enrichment offerings include lick-mats, frozen peanut butter Kongs, fruit smoothies, scent spaces, and others.

With the scent space, they often arrange them so that the dog gets to track down treats. This has worked so well that they now offer their own enrichment snacks which are homemade organic snacks which are frozen so that it takes the dogs longer to go through them. The lick bowls are made with nutritious fruits which are good for dogs.

For the appropriate breeds they offer a herding ball which is a stuffed animal on a line which recreates the experience of herding and hunting prey. On a similar note, they offer a flirt pole, which is a toy on a pole which is not tacked into the ground, which helps the dogs expel energy. On the physical side, they offer gym classes, agility courses, and walk through tunnels.

In terms of Anna Radle's experience in producing better outcomes for pets, she focuses upon the enrichment trend that has been growing over the past 6-7 years. She stresses that enrichment is key for profit in the pet care industry, and must be part of your foundation of services, and is all about providing continuously better experiences for pets.

This requires looking at individual pets, making them even more comfortable and happy, and making the experience feel personalized. A key reason why she has not currently expanded beyond the existing 150 dogs per day at her facility is that she doesn't want to expand and become so large that she cannot maintain this personalized approach.

One of Anna's favorite stories helps summarize why her teams have been so successful in providing better outcomes for pets. She had a pet guest named Suki, who was diabetic, and wasn't eating despite many attempts from her staff. Anna leaned in on her creative problem solving skills and decided to go to Chick-fil-A® Filet to buy chicken nuggets to get Suki to eat something.

She called the pet parent to ask for input and was given the okay to proceed. She then got Suki to eat the chicken nuggets, took a video of the experience, and sent it off to the pet parent to make her feel more comfortable with the happy ending. This resulted in Suki getting back to healthy mealtimes.

The client was so blown away that years later, when asked why she had been bringing all her dogs to Anna for over twenty years, she noted that Anna's team exhibited more caring than others in a very emotional business, and she sent a copy of that twenty year old video back to Anna. The results of Anna' problem solving not only returned a dog to health, but also created a raving fan, bringing countless more referrals and revenue over the years.

Matt Pepper's perspective on improving outcomes with animals in animal shelters goes back thirty years and shows lots of progress. He notes that three decades ago, Michigan Humane was merely a processing center for 60,000 animals per year. It has evolved into a trauma hospital and the only viable source available for medical help for many animals experiencing gunshot wounds, stabs, car accident trauma, etc. The facility is the last hope for countless animals.

Nevertheless, this level of care in operations, surgeries, and resources is expensive, and the costs are growing all the time.

Matt stresses that while they are striving to create an entire behavior modification program at Michigan Humane, the basis of most of it is much needed enrichment. They use much of the 100,000 hours of volunteer time every year for walking and playing with the dogs, but most animals spend 23 out of 24 hours per day in an enclosure.

To optimize this less-than-ideal reality, their volunteer groups build enrichment toys that the dogs can use in their enclosures. To sum it up, for many animals' enrichment is just as important as the medical care they provide. He stresses that you need to work on the dogs' minds to keep their future sustainable. He also points out that behavioral issues can be hard to see, so you need to use enrichment.

In the city of Detroit, they have had 5 deaths in 2 years due to dog attacks. That tightens the focus on ensuring that dogs are well-rounded pets before they are put into the community. When they determine the issue is not behavioral, but rather a temperament issue, they don't place that animal in the community. To help continue future progress in this area, he said staff need the most help in training, and veterinarians need to be educated to be better leaders.

Apryl Steele shared a lot of wisdom with stories on how to improve the outcomes with animals by focusing on behavioral training. She says every week they get more new dogs which are typically fearful.

She says some perceived these animals as aggressive, but they are just scared, and need their confidence built up. Apryl notes that behavior programs that build confidence are key, including behavioral foster homes, which include some fosters trained by her behavior team. She notes this training can transform dogs, and most dogs arriving anxious and scared are then turned around.

While this is often the case, there is always a small cohort of dangerous animals who are truly aggressive, and it is not fair to them to isolate them in a kennel for years. She cited a story in rural Colorado of a dangerous dog who jumped through a plate glass window, pounced on and mauled an innocent dog being walked on a leash with his pet parent.

The facility where this dangerous dog had been taken kept it alone by itself in a kennel where no one could touch it, no one could walk it, and it was completely isolated for seven years. She argues that this is not true animal welfare. That is a great example of Apryl's insistence that compassion, i.e. what is better for the animal, is more important than passion, i.e. what feels better to you.

Apryl also has countless cases of enrichment helping to make animals happier and healthier, while typically being better for the environment. She is especially fond of reusing materials. For example, they have volunteers making cat toys on a weekly basis using toilet paper and paper towel rolls. This results in many more cats playing and getting curious.

With dogs she loves to intentionally give them things to tear apart and chew up. For example, they play a game where they give the dogs cardboard boxes to tear up, they then clean up the mess, and afterwards have the potential adopters visit them. Her team also receives large quantities of used beds and blankets donated, which they reuse rather than letting them go into the landfill.

Dan Poirier shared a very helpful success story with us in terms of truly setting up dogs for success with better outcomes for all their pet guests attending daycare and boarding at Fetch n' Catch. He says their biggest success is launching a Day Camp Program. Like many others they started out in daycare with group play for twenty dogs in a group, organized by size.

However, they learned that approximately 50% or more of the group of twenty dogs would not succeed running around with other dogs, they would not like it, might be afraid, could become overstimulated, and some could end up being aggressive.

Despite these serious issues with some group play groups, many facilities just keep on offering them, trying to make them work out, even if this requires questionable tactics, including those as extreme as muzzling some dogs.

Dan's team knew that forcing group play on many dogs was not the right thing to do. So, they launched their Day Camp Program for dogs who do not like groups, or who don't like other dogs at all. Dan's team set this Day Camp up in a separate building next door to their standard day care. They take 60 dogs per day for Dog Camp, and each one receives a 1-for-1 session. Each staff member is assigned a certain number of dogs, and each dog gets a holistic experience for the day.

Dan also shared his P.E.T. model for dogs at his facility. "P" represents Play activity, which includes toys. "E" means exercise including treadmills, taking a walk, agility course, etc., and "T" stands for thinking which includes basic training, puzzle toys, and brain games.

When dogs benefit from the P.E.T. model, at the end of the day they are typically tired, have gotten all their energy out, they are safe, and they have not been put in a situation where they will not succeed. This, says Dan, is truly sustainable.

Related to the P.E.T. model, and as part of their enrichment program, Dan stresses it is important to have defined "proper use of equipment,' especially with toys. Before they began defining the proper use of toys, dogs would be allowed to chew on toys at anytime, anywhere, and for as long as they wanted, so they ended up destroying lots of toys fast, which was not so sustainable.

After defining the rules of "proper use of equipment" they have specific guidelines on how the dogs can play with the toy, and what games they can play with each specific toy, and for how long. Since initiating this program, they haven't had to buy new toys for many months.

When reviewing the benefits of Day Camp, the P.E.T. model, and enrichment programs there are multiple sustainability improvements benefiting the dogs, the staff, the planet, and the business. Now time is spent more purposefully and efficiently on dogs with Day Camp vs group play.

In terms of employees, staff morale has improved as there are fewer dogs with problems at Day Camp, and the staff's work is not as exhausting. In terms of business and cost savings, Dan's team now retains all those 60 dogs who enjoy Day Camp, not only for daycare, but also for boarding and grooming.

A complementary tactic that beautifully aligns with—and enhances—the enrichment strategy is clicker training for shelter cats, as implemented by Lori□Kogan and colleagues at Colorado State University and N.C.□State, and later promoted by shelters like Maddie's Fund. Kogan's 2017 study trained 100 cats using 15 short clicker sessions, teaching behaviors like target touching, sitting, spinning, and "high-five"—with 79% mastering target touching and 60% spinning—in just minutes per day[1].

Not only did cats learn new behaviors, they showed increased exploratory activity, reduced stress, and improved visibility at cage fronts—the latter linked to higher adoption potential[2].

While this complements the book's emphasis on enrichment by providing cognitive engagement and stress relief through brief, structured training, it adds measurable gains in adoption-readiness and emotional well-being—without requiring large time commitments. Integrating clicker training offers a practical, research-backed enhancement to the enrichment toolkit that directly fosters better animal outcomes.

Jess Okon believes in promoting longevity in the mindset. As an example, at a board & train facility focusing just on a 4-6 week training program, owners could also include training lessons that pet parents can use at home. These home training lessons can then act as life-long exercises for the pet parent which can be done at home.

She also notes that there is a lot of waste that is created by pet facilities if they are not careful, including using products like paper towels, and cleaning supplies used improperly. In addition to potentially hurting the environment, these can also increase costs which drive more price increases which could be avoided.

1. veterinaryevidence.org+6pubmed.ncbi.nlm.nih.gov+6chewonthis.maddiesfund.org+6.

2. chewonthis.maddiesfund.org

Happier staff = Happier animals:

Jennifer Wolf-Pierson supports most industry leaders' views that achieving better outcomes with animals must be a top industry priority. When the dogs are healthy and happy the boarding and board & train business's clients will spend more money, and for animal shelters the adoption rate will increase.

One of the cross-over relationships within sustainability is that the staff's mood totally reflects on the dogs and cats. When humans are not happy, pets will be unhappy, resulting in more veterinary visits and other costs. One of the keys to avoiding this problem is to prevent burnouts with staff, which requires increasing leaders' touch time with their staff to stay up to date on how they are doing. When you do this, the pets will notice the positive impacts in addition to the staff.

Jennifer is also a big believer in enrichment to improve the outcomes with dogs. In her case this means investing in 4-5 weeks of staff training for daycare groups. This investment pays off in spades as it reduces the time to cross train other staff members. In terms of talent development, investing in this enrichment training also is very successful as it has opened up more advancement opportunities. As these value-added enrichment activities produce happier pets, this leads to happier pet parent customers, and reduces the employee turnover rate, which further enhances outcomes with pets.

Further enrichment benefits for the staff include feeling like they have more control over their jobs, have more meaningful jobs, and have improved career development opportunities. To be clear, Dom Hodgson thinks that enrichment for the staff is as important as it for dogs. This is particularly important when it comes to offering staff a career progression track. The other positive outcomes for the businesses include that clients typically love the premium services and the outcomes for their dogs, which in turn results in the facilities making more money.

To add some interesting dimensions to how Apryl's team improves outcomes with animals, here are a few extra insights. In terms of time, they have 1,500 volunteers donating tons of time to make the animals better off. Volunteers walk dogs twice a day, and they contribute to enrichment in multiple ways including making toys.

This enrichment helps reduce the length of stay for the 20,000 animals they receive every year which is a huge plus. In terms of talent, April points out that she has great people on her team who understand animal behavior, and they form some specialized teams. Interestingly, many are former zookeepers, and these skills are great to facilitate the adoption of the animals as these team members are often better "matchmakers" because they typically understand both animals and people.

Gary Weitzman shared a great animal shelter story with us that illustrates how to do an even better job of achieving better outcomes for animals. In 2018 his team decided to accept the offer from San Diego to manage animal services for 14 cities. Adding to a base of just two cities, this was exponential growth for his team.

As he commented, most of the changes they led in this massive expansion had good outcomes, including achieving a much higher adoption rate, a big improvement in return to owner rate, introducing much better services at a quarter of the previous market price, introducing free spay and neuter services, and opening a vaccine clinic open seven days a week.

One of the challenges was that his team went from two cities where they had limited admission shelters to 14 cities where they took in all animals. This challenge meant they could not control how many animals they were taking in, which is how they ended up being at 185% of the capacity for dogs.

To continue to improve upon all the initial achievements, they now have 18 behavior trainers, a new animal care staff, a new dog day out program, and usually 12 dedicated employees at each of their five campuses for behavior and care management.

So how do the finances work for Gary's team and their clients in San Diego?

They are now doing municipal contract work and only charging 40-65% of the costs, raising the rest of the money from generous donors. For each of the 14 cities they now serve they save taxpayers somewhere between $500,000 and $10,000,000 per year. As Gary's team is "mission centric," they view this relationship with their client cities as a true win-win.

Other pet welfare improvement ideas:

Are you looking for specific sustainable solutions for enhanced dog skincare? Tired of having that boarded pet rely on expensive solutions involving veterinary involvement? Well Charlotte Biggs' facility had a dog guest with chronic skin problems that countless vet visits weren't solving.

The pet parent clients were frustrated with this ongoing problem despite many failed attempts at solving. So Charlotte's staff asked if they could change the dog's food from a nationally-advertised dry dog food to the facility's human-grade food. During a two-week boarding stay, the skin improved immensely, with new healthy fur starting to grow where before there had only been bare patches.

Not only was the dog healthier and happier with the human-grade food, but the pet parents also started buying the food, and bringing the dog back more often. The end result, happier clients, and much more revenue for years to come. This is just another example of how just feeding pets healthier food and giving them adequate clean water are effective enrichment programs in of themselves.

Dr. Josh Fischer's team's top priority is achieving better outcomes for animals under their care. Always working with very limited resources, he constantly challenges his team to do more for animal care with the resources they can muster. The organization is considering a shift in the role of animal control officers towards community policing and initiatives to reduce the number of animals brought into shelters, focusing on building relationships within the community.

Another major theme that Josh's team is pursuing is using enrichment programs to increase adoption rates. While enrichment has been around boarding facilities for years, it is a relatively new strategy for some animal shelters. Josh's team is focusing on enrichment as they recognize that socialized animals, which receive proper enrichment, are more likely to engage with people, making them more adoptable.

Ben Day has consistently focused on improving outcomes for animals. During his time as COO at IBPSA and in his ongoing work as an industry consultant, he has helped pet care facilities create emergency action plans that protect both animals and people. His approach emphasizes proactive staff training and enrichment to ensure safety and well-being.

Jerrica Owen has some great insights as to how to achieve better outcomes for animals. For starters, and perhaps obvious to some, she focuses on reducing the number of pets coming into shelters. Once the animals are in shelters, Jerrica noted that PetCo's Love Lost AI platform for pet reunification, which uses facial recognition, is a hugely positive gamechanger, helping to reunite pets with their pet parent families.

Some benefits associated with the AI program include reducing the number of animals remaining in shelters, increasing staff time that can be focused on faster reunification of the remaining pets. Other benefits include improving the efficiency of officers, increasing the connections they make with their community, reducing food and medicines costs, and lowering staff time spent on reunification.

The author would also like to introduce readers to more specific benefits of how starting a local pet ministry can help improve the outcomes with animals at all types of pet businesses. In the case of Covenant Presbyterian Church's Blessing of the Animals event in 2025, the pet ministry team invited their local partner Charlotte Mecklenburg Police Department's Animal Care and Control to the event, and gave them time to speak to the attendees.

This speaking opportunity gave Animal Care and Control the chance to recruit more volunteers, raise more money, and get more "Wishlist" gifts. All of these aspects benefited the local animal shelters as it freed up the staff's time so that they could repurpose more time to enrichment to improve their life saving plans.

Covenant's pet ministry team also provides canine therapy for mental health and other benefits at a local school for students on the spectrum, a mainstream university, and for homeless neighbors, creating more opportunities for local adoptions at shelters, and more healthy pets for local boarding and training pet businesses. These events provide great socialization learning opportunities for the pets which benefit all.

Top 10 Learnings from Chapter 2: Prioritizing Better Outcomes for Animals

1. Facility Design Impacts Lifetime Animal Health

Thoughtful placement of buildings (sunlight, airflow), water systems (rain collection, solar wells), and HVAC design greatly improve animals' physical well-being and reduce operational environmental impact. These decisions made during design are irreversible and have long-term influence on sustainability.

2. Enrichment is Essential, Not Optional

Structured enrichment (scent rooms, agility courses, toys, training games) reduces stress, supports behavioral health, and boosts adoption rates and client satisfaction. It also prevents overstimulation and improves staff morale, making enrichment key to holistic sustainability.

3. Healthier Food and Water Lead to Better Outcomes

Switching to high-quality, human-grade food and clean water improves animal skin, coat, and overall health. These changes can increase pet parent satisfaction, return business, and reduce veterinary costs.

4. Staff Wellness Directly Impacts Animal Welfare

Burnout leads to disengaged staff and unhappy pets. Leaders must maintain close contact with staff and provide training pathways to reduce turnover, create emotional alignment, and reflect well-being onto animals.

5. Group Play Doesn't Work for Every Dog

Replacing free play with individualized programs (like Day Camp and P.E.T. models) reduces behavioral issues, enriches dogs appropriately, and improves sustainability through better staff efficiency, toy longevity, and client satisfaction.

6. Smarter Cleaning Enhances Animal and Environmental Health

Upgrading from bleach and mops to wet/dry systems or electrostatic sprayers reduces chemical usage and illness outbreaks, while improving sanitation outcomes, decreasing labor time, and benefiting staff and pets alike.

7. Reduce Shelter Intake and Accelerate Reunification

Programs like AI facial recognition tools help return pets home faster, reduce length of stay, free up staff for enrichment, and cut costs for food and medicine— driving more sustainable shelter operations.

8. Animals Need Choices

Providing dogs with physical and sensory choices in kennels (e.g., heated vs. cool floor, clear vs. frosted glass) promotes calmness, reduces anxiety, and improves adoption potential, enhancing both welfare and operational outcomes.

9. Compassionate Decision-Making Prevents Suffering

Leaders must balance emotional attachment with ethical care. Euthanizing animals suffering severe behavioral issues frees resources to help others and ensures facilities focus on quality, not just quantity of life.

10. Community Engagement and Pet Ministries Support Outcomes

Involving pet ministries in therapy programs and events (like Blessing of the Animals) builds community bonds, drives shelter visibility, and opens pathways to more volunteers, donations, and adoptable animal exposure—all critical for long-term sustainability. What Gary's team did in San Diego by expanding from 2 cities to managing 14 cities their animal shelters may not be actionable in many regions, but for those where they can, this consolidation move may be worth strategically considering.

"When you put people first in a service industry, they'll find the solutions."
— *Jennifer Wolf-Pierson*, General Manager, ABC Pet Resort, Houston TX

Chapter 3: Supporting and Empowering Staff

Staff training and education:

Supporting and empowering staff is also a huge priority in Ben Day's eyes, both while at IBPSA and now ongoing as a consultant. A powerful tool that he played a role in developing while at IBPSA is a survey-based assessment designed to improve employee training and development.

Implementation of this concept is a great foundation to help facilities of all types to understand and measure where their staff is today, so that they can customize training development to be more effective going forward. These types of assessments can also help to improve education and enrichment programs through the facilities' commitment to continuous improvement and staff development which is crucial for maintaining safety and operational effectiveness.

Jerrica Owen's perspective on supporting and empowering staff is also rich. She believes strongly in the scholarships offered by NACA and ASPCA for level 1 and 2 officers training. Some of the benefits she cited from these officer scholarships and training include reducing staff burnout and turnover, increasing humane handling, improving de-escalation, reducing animal stress, enhancing communications, and lowering recruitment costs. This officers' training also directly contributes to improving enrichment for animals and allows for more staff time with animals.

In terms of success with empowering and supporting staff, Dom Hodgson also has quite a bit of experience. He cites staff burnout and turnover as huge ongoing problems. It is difficult to retain and grow people in pet care. His solution for this is also enrichment for people. His consultancy offers lots of detailed ways to improve through their product The Employee Enrichment Passport. The programs include ways to ensure employees keep learning new skills and have a career progression. This leads to more staff fulfillment, unlocking hidden staff talents, and increases their excitement with the business.

Alex Varney at Pinnacle Pet shared her successes when it came to better empowering and engaging staff. Over the past 8 years they've dealt with many of the same challenges as other pet care facilities in terms of the high turnover rates which often come with younger employees looking for "in between" jobs. Pinnacle has had great success in improving engagement and retention by creating new staff development pathways.

These are performance based and include more opportunities for raises. To start with, Pinnacle tends to focus more on career-oriented people offering better pay during the interview process, which has significantly reduced burnout and engagement problems. Their leadership pathways offer lots of career growth opportunities including options in boarding, customer service, front desk receptionist, training, and even grooming. All these efforts have also improved their culture. Some of the related enrichment benefits for staff have come from creating and supporting a video-based training program which improves the team's time efficiencies and provides a resource which can be revisited when necessary.

In terms of how Anna Radle summarizes her approach to supporting and empowering staff, she says it is all about education, specifically about teaching and sharing to help the staff grow. She considers it a success story when she helps an employee grow so well that they leave for positions of greater responsibility, and especially to lead their own business.

For example, a former manager of hers, Megan, left in 2024 to be General Manager of another pet care facility and has been experiencing success thanks to what she learned from Anna, especially in terms of problem solving. Anna stresses that leaders must be engaged with the staff, as they are the "crux of your business." She also says that enrichment for pets also plays a key role in helping her employees as well. Important on both fronts, Anna recommends that facilities keep lines of communication open with clients on all they are doing with enrichment and staff training to create positive impressions, good experiences and to build relationships.

Anna also has a lot of wisdom to share when summarizing the challenges facing people in pet care today. Tenacity is how she describes how she keeps going, meaning sucking it up in the face of challenges, and working through those challenges, and above all staying positive. To do this, you must be open-minded and education-driven to survive as an entrepreneur, and even more to thrive.

Dianna Starr's perspective on supporting and empowering staff also ties to education. Specifically, she encourages all pet business owners to invest in educational seminars and conferences. Whether they offer continuing educational credits or not, she says these educational opportunities are fundamental to your success with your team.

She also encourages owners to empower their staff to continuously enroll in these training programs. When travel makes trade shows too expensive, she coaches people to take online courses. This training will pay off. What is curious to the author is despite the great wisdom of Dianna, Anna and others focusing on employee education, the vast majority of pet care facilities do not do this.

How does the author come to that conclusion?

As he attends many pet industry educational conferences each year, both for boarding facilities and animal shelters, the attendance numbers are tiny vs. the known number of people employed in those types of businesses. Small wonder that there are so many pet care businesses struggling these days.

Matt Pepper's team at Michigan Humane has been innovating to improve the sustainability of empowering staff. Three years ago they set up a training program for licensed vet techs. Their donors offered to pay the tuition, but nobody entered the program, as the vet tech hopefuls couldn't afford to leave their day job where they earned wages to support their families.

Rather than give up, Matt's team approached Penn Foster (an online training resource) to run the training, got the donors to pay the cost, gave each student a mentor, controlled the students practical experience, and gave them a full-time job working for Michigan Humane so they could afford to continue supporting their families. 60% are minority candidates. When they graduate, they tend to stay in the community, so this benefits the community long term and creates a sustainable employee base for Matt's team.

When Michigan Humane started this program, there were 13 applicants in the first year. This year, they got 200 applicants from 49 different universities from all over the country to apply for 15 of these slots. Also worth mentioning is that this program was designed for vet techs in years one or two of school, which also helped them do better in years 3 and 4.

In terms of supporting and empowering staff, Gary Weitzman cites San Diego's Humane Society's "culture of care," which they have been doing for about a dozen years. In their culture, the priority is to take care of the staff first. For the last 5 years, they have been voted a top place to work, both in San Diego and nationally, based on input from their own team.

To support this unique culture with their 700+ employees they started a Leadership Program, which includes a Learning Academy for managers and directors.

As approximately 70% or more of the staff is under 30 years old, this leadership training is important to retain and grow their staff. Additionally, they have started a mentor/mentee program, as well as a sabbatical program for all those who have been there for 10+ years, where veteran employees qualify for a month off to do anything except work.

In terms of what a local Pet Ministry can do to help local pet businesses better support and empower staff at animal shelters and for-profit pet businesses, there are many aspects. Some examples from Covenant's Pet Ministry outreach include educating local pet parents on the benefits of pet socialization using training from a presentation with a local Veterinarian, which not only leads to better pet health, but more business and jobs for local trainers and boarding/daycare facilities.

Another typical example is that when the Pet Ministry invites their local Animal Care & Control team to speak to recruit more volunteers, the resultant increase in number of volunteers relieves some of the time staff spend on various activities and empowers them to allocate more time to enrichment.

Dan Poirier points out that staff retention is a challenge across the industry, so having sustainable plans for supporting and empowering staff are key. He says the number one frustration with staff is lack of confidence in their jobs. Essentially, staff often do not know how good they are doing. To prevent and fix these issues, he says you need transparent training systems and strong facility leadership to point staff in the right direction.

The reason he and Mal developed and launched PACKPRO as an online staff training program was that after developing successful programs for over eight to ten years at Fetch n' Catch, they knew they could help others in the industry strengthen their skills in this area. Some benefits of the training system include that once the new employee has invested two weeks in this tailored training program, they are ready to hit the ground running, be more confident, and be compliant with other staff.

Using this system also benefits the facility, as management now uses proactive leadership, not reactive management. All of this improves staff retention, avoids the approximate cost of $1500 to hire and train someone else to replace the one leaving. So, in an industry that very often has annual turnover rates of 100%, Dan gets to retain most of his 60 staff from year to year.

Empower the staff to take charge:

Apryl Steele is also a big supporter of supporting and empowering staff. When she started in her role as CEO at Humane Colorado (HC), the decision-making process already in place for a while was hierarchical and black and white. She said the guidelines in place were adequate but were not so helpful in encouraging and aiding staff to make their own decisions when appropriate or necessary under specific situations.

She wanted to change this culture, but it was hard and it took her seven or eight years to make the changes stick. People who wanted empowerment had not liked the former black and white hierarchical rules, and had already left the organization, thus they were already gone when she arrived. As such, virtually everyone in the place when she started liked black and white, and being told what to do. When Apryl started to change the culture, this made lots of people uncomfortable. Then she had to teach the staff the skills to make them confident in making their own decisions.

Some employees did leave, as they wanted a return to their black and white world. As a result, Apryl has invested a lot of time and money in leadership training. Her leadership 101 training takes over 20 hours per month, and the duration is over a year. The goals of the training are to train her team on how to have courageous conversations, how to think critically, and how, through the processes, to become more joyful and comfortable with their new empowerment.

Apryl's changes to better support and empower staff also benefited their operations in terms of enrichment and improving morale. HC staff had been suffering a lot of burnout. Many jobs were defined as having four ten-hour days feeding animals and cleaning kennels. So Apryl changed this to support the culture and staff engagement they could benefit from going forward.

She also changed the job to three ten-hour days feeding animals and cleaning kennels, and on the fourth day the employee is responsible for making the animals joyful! To accomplish that, employees spent more time going around, interacting with the animals, and figuring out how to make them sustainably more joyful.

To increase the odds of success, the staff also collaborated with the enrichment coordinator. Together they became very creative, successful, and joyful themselves in the process. They figured out how to be new and innovative with puzzle toys and food, and the process led to the dogs getting more special attention.

Some of the toughest types of problems to solve can be those created through facilities designed without attention to potential negative impacts on the operational side. As an example, at Charlotte Biggs' facility in Texas, the sun in the hot summer was making it really difficult for the dogs to spend enough time outdoors with their enrichment activities, and causing heat exhaustion.

So, she empowered the staff to come up with a solution. They came up with a fix that worked wonderfully. First, they changed the rotation of buildings where the dogs spent time, so that each of the buildings where they spent time were used during times when they were mostly in the shade when the dogs were occupying them. They also bought sun tents, or shades, to cover the outdoor areas receiving the most sun. In this way, they were able to increase enrichment time for any dog that wanted it.

With respect to the talent/staff, this significantly increased motivation, engagement, and ownership. The financial impact included happier staff, improved team retention, and then increased return pet visits. So, a true win-win-win!

Mark Klaiman shares some great stories about supporting and empowering staff, which also overlap with other sustainability benefits. The team divides waste into compostable, recyclable, and true waste. This enables the facility to benefit from diversion credits where the greener they are, the more money they save, versus adding more stuff to waste, which costs more. Also, he put his managers in charge of compliance ensuring that the staff puts the correct type of materials in the correctly colored can, as their waste management company checks this.

In other words, if you put waste into recycling or compost, there are negative financial consequences. He laughed, telling this story, as when their team does it wrong, the manager must do a 'dumpster dive' to check how they sort materials. As the dumpsters are large and gross, it only takes one dumpster dive to motivate a manager to get his/her team back in line.

Not only does this approach save money and reduce environmental waste, it also saves the team a lot of time. A special bonus they have because of their geographic location is that their composting facility is a biomass facility, which means it can also compost dog waste. This saves his company even more time and money.

Eve Molzhon is also a big proponent of supporting and empowering staff. She shared a great story with us about how her staff came up with some great new plans to improve enrichment by researching and innovating from learnings on how sounds can impact dogs.

They also researched the costs. After some initial research they found that noisy environments were not only causing a lot of stress for the dogs, but that this was leading to far more incidences of diarrhea, which then means spending a lot more on paper towels, plastic bags, and staff time to pick it up. Not surprisingly, this also hurts employee retention. Eve's empowered staff then did more research on sound's impact on the business both indoors and outdoors.

Indoors, Eve's team learned that dogs are much quieter, with half of the lights turned off. Adding soothing reggae music enhanced this calming effect.

So now every day from 10:00 - 10:30 AM half the lights are turned off indoors, and the music comes on. The reggae music learning is that it is soothing to dogs with no crescendos and decrescendos. This monotone, even rhythm soothes the dogs, and they bark less for less noise. Specifically, doing this reduced noise pollution by 40% and reduced the electricity bill!

Outdoors, Eve's staff determined that sounds of life in this urban area created a fair amount of noise and stress on dogs. The team was successful in desensitizing the dogs to these outdoors noises by playing recordings of similar sounds indoors before they went outside to experience good things during playtime, potty breaks, etc.

They also further reduced the impact of outdoor noises by buying shower curtains and hanging them on the outdoors chain link fences. The shower curtains acted as both sound and sight barriers, resulting in lower noise and fewer dogs barking. Thus Dog Handler Academy's approach was successful in desensitizing the dogs so they didn't get as stressed hearing noise outside. Furthermore, the shower curtains were only $10-$15 each, serving as inexpensive barriers. Finally, the staff had much less diarrhea to pick up outside, and the dogs were much happier.

Three other innovations of Eve's staff empowering research work helped them improve the sustainability of their business, this time again in enrichment, and centered around well-known sound-related issues around Memorial Day, July 4th, and Halloween. In terms of Memorial Day and the 4th of July what Eve's team discovered is that when they proactively played indoors recorded sounds of fireworks before the dogs went out to fun activities and going potty, and then nothing bad happened, they successfully desensitized the dogs to the sounds of fireworks. Later when the dogs returned home, they had lots of clients comment on how much better the dogs tolerated the sound of fireworks.

With Halloween, Eve's team played recordings of either doorbells ringing and/or kids saying trick or treat indoors right before the dogs went out for fun. Again, when the dogs were later at home with their families, they remained much calmer and happier when they experienced October 31st with their families. The clients picked up on this, and thanked Eve's team for the help. They understood that by playing recordings of fireworks and the doorbell right before a happy time, it benefited everyone.

Building a culture:

Jennifer Wolf-Pierson's focus on supporting and empowering staff also brought to light some unique valuable management insights. Consistent with some of my mentors, Jennifer believes strongly in when you meet someone with great potential, that you design and craft a job just for that person, as it gets them into your team for future growth. In one case she hired a new person who had just moved from out of state and gave him a job as maintenance manager just to get started.

By applying a high touch approach in managing him she got to know him by listening to, hearing his stories, and building a relationship. Through this process, Jennifer learned that he and his wife were struggling with a child on the spectrum. So, she then introduced him to their office manager who had similar issues with her children, demonstrating that management cared about his family.

This personal touch really motivated him to grow in so many ways, to work harder, and to bring more creative solutions to the business' problems. He has been promoted several times and now manages all the activity departments by leveraging his growing work ethic, being a role model of accountability, and caring for others. This story totally underscores Jennifer's management style of putting people first in a service industry, and then letting the people find the solutions.

Jennifer also stresses that to get the best overall sustainable results with your staff you need to pay a living wage or even higher. Gone are the days when you could pay just a minimum wage or slightly higher. If you hire people at these levels, they won't stay, and you will end up paying a lot of money on employee turnover and re-training.

She said she learned this lesson when she calculated that one year her team spent $120,000 on employee turnover costs. Since then, her average wages have gone from $9 per hour to around $17 per hour. In doing this, the employee turnover has dramatically decreased, the pets are happier, the pet parent customers are happier, her teams are more engaged, and she has a much lower amount spent on employee turnover.

For Jennifer, one of the most important insights is that all of pet care is a service business run by humans, and prioritizing and focusing on higher touch initiatives with humanity is the key to being sustainable. This is what got her business to survive the 1990s, and what will ensure it is still viable in 30 years.

This high touch approach needs to be combined with constantly trying new things to ensure innovation and staff engagement remain strong. Especially for the boarding businesses which are "mom and pop," this high touch human approach will be even more important as they compete with large private-equity industry consolidators who have deeper pockets.

Jennifer further emphasizes that the future success of boarding involves a shift in mindset to where staff are truly becoming professionals. These pet professionals will need continuous education, training, and certifications to keep the businesses competitive. To do well in this area, which also applies to all areas of pet care, means investing in going to industry conferences, not just to go to classes, but to network, and talking to industry vendors/exhibitors who are bringing innovation to the market. Doing this and becoming an early adopter of sustainable innovations will help keep you moving forward.

Jess Okon's team's success in moving to automated meter dispensing systems for cleaning supplies also had a big positive impact on empowering and engaging staff. By saving labor time, they were able to repurpose this time to more training time, including higher level and enrichment training. This resulted in happier staff, happier dogs, and less employee turnover. Moreover, it provided more time to focus on career progression and resulted in a happier team overall.

Dr. Josh Fisher also suggests that facilities should create a culture that welcomes pilot programs and experimentation, leading to a proactive approach to implementing changes and addressing resistance. As is true for all types of pet businesses, it is critical to engage staff in the change process.

Importantly, that means asking for staff's input, rather than telling them what to do. This is where pilot programs and experimentation come in very handy. Another key benefit of this approach is that it helps prevent stagnation and encourages ongoing development.

Supporting and empowering staff to improve processes is a core strategy for Dr. Fisher's team in Charlotte's Animal Care and Control. One of the concepts that Josh's team excels at compared, not only to other animal shelters but also to boarding facilities, is emphasizing the importance of staff time as a valuable resource. In many cases for both shelters and boarding facilities, as staff expenses are the biggest line item, this can have huge positive outcomes.

While we will talk about this again, it is key to do time studies to truly optimize your staff's duties to be as efficient as possible. I have seen all types of leaders of pet businesses who believe they know how their staff spends their time, but who are totally shocked when they finally do time studies. One of the key benefits of time studies is that it shows you where you can save time and repurpose it elsewhere, especially toward enrichment which produces better outcomes for animals in boarding facilities, and also especially importantly at animal shelters where it increases adoption rates.

Other approaches:

A compelling complementary tactic to enhance the "supporting and empowering staff" chapter is to implement flexible, self-managed scheduling technology. For example, businesses using workforce management platforms can empower employees with a level of "gig-like schedule flexibility and control"—letting them swap shifts, define availability, and manage preferences directly via a mobile app—while managers can ensure appropriate coverage and compliance.

This tactic complements existing initiatives by significantly reducing administrative burdens, giving the staff more ownership over their time, and aligning with the ethos of empowerment seen in Charlotte Biggs' shade-rotation solution and Jennifer Wolf-Pierson's personalized roles. Staff feel trusted and valued, which boosts morale and retention.

Plus, it directly frees up leadership time to engage more meaningfully with teams, just as Dan Poirier and Jennifer emphasize. In short, self-scheduling tech is a strategic tool that can turn scheduling from a pain point into a source of empowerment—benefiting people, pets, and business.

Top 10 Learnings from Chapter 3: Supporting and Empowering Staff

1. Empower Staff to Solve Operational Problems

Involving staff in problem-solving, like addressing heat stress with shade structures, builds engagement, motivation, and ownership. This boosts retention, reduces operational disruption, and increases enrichment opportunities for pets.

2. Invest in Living Wages and Career Pathways

Paying above-minimum wages and creating advancement tracks (as with Jennifer Wolf-Pierson and Alex Varney's approaches) drastically reduce turnover. This sustains institutional knowledge, improves pet care, and increases employee morale, enhancing overall service quality.

3. Use Time Studies to Optimize Efficiency

Josh Fischer's emphasis on time studies reveals how staff time is truly used. This allows leaders to streamline tasks, repurpose hours to enrichment or training, and reduce operational waste—boosting both productivity and animal outcomes.

4. Promote Pilot Programs and Staff-Led Innovation

Encouraging experimentation and piloting changes (Josh Fischer, Eve Molzhon) avoids stagnation, fosters adaptive thinking, and leads to custom solutions that improve daily processes and increase job satisfaction.

5. Provide Personalized Roles and Emotional Support

Jenn's story of designing a job around a new hire and connecting him to colleagues with shared challenges illustrates that emotional investment leads to professional growth, increased loyalty, and a more resilient, empowered team.

6. Adopt Self-Managed Scheduling Tools

Using apps allows staff to manage their schedules, swap shifts, and set preferences. This increases flexibility and autonomy, reduces scheduling conflicts, improves morale, and saves managers time, allowing more focus on leadership and training.

7. Implement Education-First Cultures

Leaders like Anna Radle, Dianna Starr, and Matt Pepper show that supporting staff education— whether through online training, mentorships, or conference attendance—builds skills, deepens retention, and strengthens the pet care workforce pipeline.

For larger facilities like Gary Weitzman's San Diego Humane Society's "culture of care" this is a great example of how to retain and train staff through extensive programs including leadership training, mentor programs, and sabbaticals.

8. Use Sound and Environment Design to Reduce Stress

Eve Molzhon's team used sound therapy and environmental adjustments (e.g., reggae music, light dimming, outdoor noise desensitization) to calm dogs, reduce diarrhea, and improve staff efficiency—lowering both medical and labor costs.

9. Redesign Jobs to Include Joy and Enrichment

Apryl Steele changed kennel job structures to include one day focused on joy and enrichment for pets. This lowered burnout, sparked innovation in enrichment activities, and improved both employee and animal well-being.

10. Leverage External Support (e.g., Pet Ministries)

Partnering with community initiatives like pet ministries reduces staff workloads, brings in volunteers, and creates community outreach that boosts shelter visibility and business opportunities—freeing up internal resources for more impactful work.

"In most instances, the best way to save money is to be environmentally focused."
— *Mark Klaiman*, Founder and Co-Owner of Pet Camp, San Francisco

Chapter 4: Protecting the Environment

There are numerous ways to protect the environment. Don't have an unlimited budget? Start small. The environment can be protected and improved through various approaches to water use, electricity/solar usage, use of building materials, implementing recycling, and judicious use of cleaning materials.

Water:

What a lot of people don't realize is that very often doing something right for the environment can also benefit the animals and staff, and also bring cost savings and better financial results. So, while the following tactic was originally carried out to protect mother earth, it brought better outcomes all over the place.

For instance, Charlotte Biggs' pet resort in Texas was located in a place where there was no access to municipal water and wells were prohibitively expensive to drill, as a result the only viable option was to design and build a rainwater harvesting system. Another challenge was how to define the Standard Operating Procedures so that the pet resort always had enough water for their needs.

Well, they did a great job, including training staff to clean enclosures spraying from the top down, which not only prevented pathogens from splattering around with the water, but enabled them to clean the same place with much less water. Some of the impacts included less time cleaning, better enrichment through higher quality water, and a better bottom line.

Jennifer Wolf Pierson also believes strongly in protecting the environment. One of her key focuses is on finding ways to save water as her area in Houston, TX has experienced many droughts over the years. For example, in 2023 a drought ended up killing 22 trees on ABC Pet Resort's property.

One of her team's focuses on saving water has been switching away from mopping to cleaning with vacuum systems as mopping leads to excessive amounts of water running to septic or sewer which is a lot of waste. Switching to vacuum systems to clean reduced water usage by 75%, reduced overuse of chemicals by up to 75%, reduced humidity, and very importantly made the entire building smell like a place you would like to spend time in versus an old-fashioned kennel that smells like wet dogs or urine. Importantly this change has also consistently reduced the number of staff members needed to clean by one to two people.

Obviously, all these lessons of switching from mops and drains to vacuum systems apply not only to boarding facilities but to all types of facilities, including shelters.

At Brad Shear's animal shelter in RI, when they are cleaning, they use two passes of water to clean some areas instead of the three or four typically used. He points out shelters that are maybe using a detergent and bleach are going to use an additional round of spraying down every kennel versus someone who can use a single cleaner that's more environmentally friendly and maybe more effective.

For example, his team uses a Virox product called Rescue, which advertises as being more environmentally friendly once it goes down the drain, and also says is more effective in terms of water use and dilution.

At his Colorado shelter, Brad was lucky in that Boulder is in the mountains. Unlike most other places, it has plentiful water because the town owns a glacier, where most of the water comes from.

However, typical animal shelters are very water-intensive businesses as they usually wash the kennels by hosing them down,

Solar and Electric:

Another great pioneer in sustainability for pet boarding facilities is Mark Klaiman, the owner of Pet Camp in San Francisco. Mark is a big believer in designing sustainability into facilities, processes and procedures from the very beginning, which is a point in time when you have the most flexibility to make an impact. He and his wife Virginia opened in 1987 after both leaving jobs with the EPA, so they already knew a lot about sustainability.

At his first location, they planned 252 solar panels, the largest amount in San Francisco at the time. They also planned to have more efficient 220 Volts, vs. 110 Volts. He also installed a lot of LED lights which typically last around 20 years, saving both electricity and money along the way. Very importantly, he asserts that while there certainly are startup costs, in most instances the best way to save money is to be environmentally focused. He also notes that the ROIs are typically attractive.

In terms of protecting the environment, Gary's team in San Diego offers some effective programs. The wildlife program where they take care of thousands of injured animals each year is inspiring and could be replicated at more animal shelters around the country. The shelter world encompasses more than just pets, and proper management of wildlife also impacts on the environment that we all inhabit.

Their commitment to solar power is also inspiring, where all new buildings and structures must include solar power. Naming the former owner of a solar company their Facilities Director was a stroke of genius for those committed to alternative energy programs.

In terms of protecting the environment, one of Dom's UK clients was one of the first in that country to introduce electric vans for drop-offs and pick-ups for boarding/daycare. As they introduced the vans with government support, this initiative not only further increased the sustainability aura around its brand, but also saved them lots of money. This client also tied in the feature very well with premium-priced subscription service packages, further increasing the funds to build an environmentally focused brand.

Recycling/ Reusing:

Dr. Josh Fisher's team also takes a holistic approach in protecting the environment related to their animal shelter. The team recognized the necessity of prioritizing sustainability in the facility's design and construction, indicating a shift from a purely cost-focused approach to one that integrates sustainable practices. On the operational side, their team has explored recyclable options for litter boxes and scratching posts.

Josh also suggests that animal welfare professionals should actively engage with municipalities' sustainability goals, advocating for alignment between animal welfare initiatives and environmental sustainability efforts to gain support from elected officials. He also suggests reaching out to sustainability and resilience officers in local governments for interviews, emphasizing their unique perspective on integrating sustainability into various aspects of operation.

Anna Radle has a great story to share about protecting the environment, which could help many other pet care facilities. She calls it Turf. Many years ago, she says that many pet care facilities used mulch, hay, and in her case pea gravel to cover their outdoor play areas. There were all sorts of problems with those approaches, hence a growing trend to install artificial turf these days, however it was too expensive for Anna's team to afford.

One day while driving Anna noticed that the local high school was tearing up the turf on their football field to replace it with newer turf. After speaking with many folks, she met the contractor removing the old turf, and asked if she could buy it from him to use at her pet care facility. The contractor decided to give it to her for free as this would save him lots of money by not having to transport it away and pay landfill fees.

Anna transformed her pea gravel play yard to a new one covered in turf that drained well and the dogs loved, aka a huge win at recycling/reusing. This was also a Game Changer for her business as it kept the dogs cleaner, they didn't bring gravel inside, and saved labor time and money cleaning the dogs. In addition to saving lots of time and money, she loves how much this is reducing environmental waste as well, as she kept all this turf out of the landfill.

Dan Poirier also cited some enrichment programs which contribute to protecting the planet. For example, as mentioned earlier in the book, the "proper use of equipment" for toys has significantly reduced the rate at which they need to replace toys.

Also, the systemized processes save them time. This is especially so with the chemical dilution measurements that ensure they are not using chemicals as quickly as previously, reduces the amounts of chemicals used, and goes over well with the young staffers who really appreciate these improvements to deliver a better work environment. In terms of cost savings, these programs save money on utilities, water, and other areas which are reinvested back into taking better care of dogs, the staff, and the business.

Cleaning supplies and building design:

In terms of protecting the environment, Alex Varney stresses that if it is within your budget, you can enjoy a lot of benefits by building your own customized space. She is happy with their facility HVAC which was originally built for them with a focus on oversized air systems to improve air flow and to recycle airflow. They also designed the building to have skylights which enables them to turn off lights at certain times, thus saving energy.

The skylights are also a positive factor for the dogs as they reduce stress and noise. Their facility is also designed with big overhead doors to let in more natural air. She also stresses that utilizing the outdoors as often as possible can provide all sorts of benefits which the dogs enjoy such as exploration and sound and scent stimulation. Alex emphasizes that if you want to save on time, do the design and build job right the first time, as this will save you lots of time down the road.

She notes that you will get a lot of benefits out of educating your employees and clients as to why and how you designed your facility to protect the environment. While on the topic of eco-friendly Alex also reports that she has good experiences with UV lights and air purifiers which both the staff and the dogs have reacted positively to as well.

Mark Klaiman suggests that every pet/animal care facility can do more in terms of protecting the planet. At the top of his list, he suggests that everyone do a feasibility study with Solar panels, and also solar thermal. He also says to stop using hoses, which will save lots of water and money. He notes that each year more and more ecofriendly building materials are available, many of which deliver benefits across many areas of sustainability.

One of the coolest features he shared with us is that some of his facilities have retractable glass roofs, that not only bring in so much fresh air which the dogs love, but also sunlight which can be a great natural disinfectant.

Dianna Starr's view on protecting the environment also centers on her expertise in wet/dry cleaning systems. She points out that it starts with the architects during the design phase, and then goes down to the contractors to ensure they choose sustainable materials that are appropriate for pet care facilities.

By working with a progressive vision and team, and staying away from old school mindsets of drains, bleach, and mops, but instead choosing the right HVAC systems and air cleaning systems you will not only reduce pet outbreaks, but also reduce the amount of water used and lower the sewer impact.

Scott Learned emphasizes that it is not enough to hire an "eco-friendly" building architect or designer if they don't know what is appropriate for animals, and unfortunately quite a few of them only know what works for humans, and not animals. As an example, he was called in to mediate a brand new building that was built in Boston for animal care by a local architect who knew lots about materials that can be green for humans, but which are bad for animals.

Some of the mistakes made with good intentions included having lots of wood indoors which dogs would chew on, and having reground asphalt for ground cover which ended up irritating the dogs' paws. Perhaps the worst mistake for dogs was that it had a vegetative roof designed to cool the building, but which instead didn't offer enough air flow, and leaked tons of water. So, the lesson learned is to be sure the team designing and building a new facility for you are experts on animal needs, and not humans.

Starting out 30 years ago when Brad Shear started at an animal shelter in Boulder, they had an "aha" moment that nobody was going to walk down the hall to the one recycling bin on the floor with one piece of paper. Instead, they installed separate recycling bins next to every desk.

This vision became more important as every day there were a lot of shipping boxes received as well, and now every desk had a place for recycling cardboard.

Living and working in Colorado also means that Apryl Steele's team values protecting the environment as a key part of their sustainability plans. When they did a $43 million renovation of the shelter a few years ago, environmental improvements were near the top of the list of priorities.

Obviously, this included switching to LED lighting, new HVAC systems, etc. Apryl stressed one of the improvements with some of the biggest environmental changes was something pretty basic. Previously each kennel had a trench drain in the back. To clean it the staff sprayed the poop until it dissolved into the drain, which in addition to taking quite a while, used a lot of water and was not always highly effective in sanitation. The new design has a clinical sink – which basically looks like a big square toilet without a seat.

Now the staff pick up the poop with scoopers, and flush it away in floor-mounted service sinks with jet flow action. The sinks serve as "communal toilets" for the shelter's canine waste as well as leftover dog food. "They greatly minimize the odors normally associated with shelter cleaning," says director of strategic initiatives Linda Yarbrough.

Dan's team at Fetch n' Catch also believes in protecting the environment, and this idea is gaining momentum. He believes that there are lots of little things to do to help in this area. They use compostable poop bags to pick up poop, chemical dilution systems to use less product, and LED lighting for high efficiency. He says they continue to get new ideas from some of the younger employees who care a lot about the environment.

Over 12 years ago, Eve Mohlson toured 22 pet resorts in 3 states to learn how they were doing pet care. She asked them all two questions. If you had to do it all over again, what wouldn't you do? The second question was what is the one thing that you rock at doing?

As she didn't have a job, she could not get a loan. So instead, she took out 12 credit cards and got $50,000 without knowing how much she really needed, and signed a lease to rent a 15,000 square foot warehouse. To prioritize where to start building, and as she lives in Wisconsin where it gets really cold, she decided to start building in the areas in the warehouse nearest the water pipes, and to heat these areas.

That is how she began, with a 6,500 square foot area inside the warehouse which included one furnace and one bathroom. To furnish this space it for the minimum amount of money, she spoke with two local car dealers down the road who needed to do renovation work, and she told them that if, when it was time to dispose of their old buildings' furnishings, they put them beside, and not in the dumpster, they would not have to pay someone to haul them away, and she would do so for free.

This saved the two car dealerships a lot of money, and Eve got for free perfectly good used doors, door handles, exit signs, and many other old but perfectly good furnishings for free. Her repurpose and recycle approach partnering with two car dealers enabled her to, in 72 days and for $55,000, build her brand new 6,500 square foot pet resort.

Eve's definition of sustainability in pet care has 3 components. These are "recycle and repurpose," homeopathic care, and efficiencies. Her work with the two car dealers is a great example of recycling and repurpose. Homeopathic care includes using the right chemicals and the associated correct amounts, and working correctly given animal's and people's site, sound, and smell. Efficiencies in so many different areas including design to ensure that equipment is located close to where it will be needed.

In terms of protecting the environment, Eve Molzhon's team is very proactive, especially when it comes to building design. When building a new facility recently Eve decided upfront to reduce waste related to plumbing with a hub design approach. Specifically, they decided that all the functions that use water are in one area. One wall is for grooming, one wall is for laundry, one wall is a slip sink, and one wall houses a bathroom.

Taking this approach reduced plumbing costs, and reduced plumbing fixture costs. On a similar note they designed the new facility so that everything that was needed for each key activity was built right where it needed to be, so staff don't have to walk far for everything. They also decided to use glass blocks to let in natural lights even when they turn off the lights to reduce noise from 10-10:30am each day.

Another design learning they had was to make some halls 6 feet wide, instead of the standard 4, so that much enrichment activity can happen in these hallway areas. In these extra-large hallways they have jumps, fit-paw equipment, and also have space for some dog training.

A valuable complementary tactic that aligns beautifully with Chapter 4's focus on environmental stewardship is the implementation of **rain gardens or bioswales** around pet care facilities—an approach already used by zoos and public parks to manage stormwater naturally. For example, the Rogers Bridge "Chattapoochee" Dog Park in Duluth, GA, incorporates a rain garden and bioswale to capture stormwater and control runoff, improve water quality, and add aesthetic green space for dogs and humans alike (see tsw-design.com). Similarly, the Cincinnati Zoo captures rainwater on-site to reduce water use and save costs, collecting over a billion gallons so far via harvesting systems (arcsainternational.org).

These green infrastructure features not only filter pollutants and recharge groundwater, but also create enriching, natural outdoor environments—enhancing animal welfare, supporting biodiversity, reducing flooding risk, and saving on utility bills. By integrating rain gardens or bioswales into facility landscapes, pet care operations can effectively complement existing water conservation and habitat initiatives, offering improved environmental impact with added enrichment for pets and staff.

More ideas:

Jess Okon team's success in moving to automated metered dispenser systems for cleaning supplies also helped protect the environment. By properly diluting highly-concentrated cleaning supplies/chemicals back to the desired strength and the correct water dilution ratio, her facility reduced the number of times a staff member needed to rinse off surfaces, and also reduced the amount of chemicals going down the drain during a certain period of time.

This also led to more improvements in enrichment as they had an overall cleaner and healthier facility. When customers entered they did not encounter off-putting chemical smells. The dogs with their super sensitive noses were also able to avoid harsh chemical smells, which made them happier.

Ben Day's philosophy importantly includes an emphasis on protecting the environment. Given his training and educational focus Ben stresses the importance of doing this to enhance the quality of life for future generations. In the short term, Ben stresses the importance of engaging today's employees in discussions on the environment to ensure more impact now and down the road.

As many animal shelters depend on raising funds from donors, Matt Pepper pointed out something that several others have mentioned to the author. It is very important to have environmental programs in place because this is a very important issue for the growing base of environmentally savvy donors. Not only do the facilities need to have these green programs in place, but they also need to educate as to how they benefit the community on an ongoing basis.

Many of the activities which local pet ministries promote can in some unexpected ways help protect the local environment while benefiting all sorts of local pet businesses. Whether it is providing canine therapy to local students or homeless neighbors, educating pet parents on socialization and training, and/or putting on a Blessing of the Animals event, all these activities inspire people to spend more time with their and others' pets, including spending more time walking their dogs and themselves, rather than driving a vehicle. These activities also promote more local adoptions and more pet parent investments in local dog training and/or boarding/daycare.

Top 10 Sustainability Learnings from Chapter 4: Protecting the Environment

1. Design with Environmental Sustainability from the Start

Facilities like Pet Camp, San Diego Humane Society's new buildings, and Apryl Steele's shelter showcase the long-term benefits of integrating eco-conscious design features—solar panels, LED lighting, HVAC upgrades, and clinical sinks—at the construction phase. This leads to reduced utility costs, lower environmental impact, and provides healthier, more efficient environments for pets and people.

2. Implement Water-Saving Cleaning Methods

Switching from hoses and mops to vacuum systems and clinical sinks, as seen at ABC Pet Resort and Apryl Steele's shelter, reduces water waste by up to 75%, decreases chemical use, improves sanitation, and saves staff labor hours—thereby improving environmental and financial outcomes.

3. Harvest and Reuse Rainwater

Charlotte Biggs' rainwater harvesting system demonstrates how off-grid water solutions can provide operational autonomy, reduce water bills, and improve animal care by offering high-quality water. Training staff on efficient use maximizes these benefits.

4. Use Repurposed or Recycled Materials

Anna Radle's creative reuse of turf from a local high school significantly reduced landfill waste and cut cleaning costs while providing a cleaner and more enjoyable outdoor space for pets, proving that recycling can drive sustainability and enrichment simultaneously.

5. Adopt Automated Dilution and Dispenser Systems

Jess Okon's implementation of cleaning supply dispensers ensures accurate dilution, reducing waste and chemical exposure for pets and staff. This enhances environmental safety and supports enrichment by maintaining a fresher, healthier facility atmosphere.

6. Leverage Facility Design for Natural Light and Airflow

Alex Varney's and Eve Molzhon's use of skylights, wide hallways, UV filters, glass blocks, and airflow-focused HVAC systems improves air quality and reduces energy use while boosting enrichment and overall pet comfort.

7. Partner with Local Governments and Experts

Dr. Josh Fisher emphasizes alignment with municipal sustainability plans and partnerships with resiliency officers. This not only secures political and funding support but integrates pet care into broader environmental and community resilience efforts.

8. Educate Staff and Community on Green Practices

Ben Day, Dianna Starr, and Dan Poirier show that staff engagement and ongoing education about green practices (like proper chemical dilution and toy care) build a culture of environmental responsibility, lowering waste and improving operational efficiency.

9. Innovate Through Green Transportation and Subscriptions

Dom's UK client's use of electric vans supported by government grants, alongside premium eco-friendly service subscriptions, reduces carbon emissions and increases revenue—building brand credibility and customer loyalty around sustainability.

10. Incorporate Green Infrastructure like Rain Gardens and Bioswales

Inspired by dog parks and zoos, rain gardens and bioswales manage runoff, improve water quality, and create attractive, enriching environments. They reduce flooding, save money, and enhance pet and staff wellness—aligning well with rainwater and design strategies already used in leading pet care facilities.

These top 10 learnings underscore that sustainability in pet care is not only good for the planet, but also a driver of better operations, happier pets and staff, and improved financial performance.

"You can't manage what you don't measure—time studies are the foundation of operational sustainability."
— *Jess Okon*, Pet Industry Consultant and Conference Speaker

Chapter 5: Achieving Time and Cost Savings

How much time are you really spending?

The author has been in the pet care industry for over 12 years, and one of his learnings is that time is your most precious resource, regardless of the type of pet business you are in, both with for-profit and non-profit businesses. As such, the author has done a fair amount of research, and would recommend that all types of pet businesses make it a priority to create and use time studies to increase operational efficiencies.

You may be starting with the challenge that you are paying staff to do tasks that either don't bring in money and/or that are low value-added tasks that don't add to your mission. When you do time studies, you can find solutions that either cut costs and let you generate more revenue with the same staff and/or allow you to refocus your staff on higher value-added enrichment to improve pet health, or even save more pet lives.

Here are five reasons to do a time study.

1. You will empower your team to do better schedule planning, and in some cases improve the prices of services.
2. You will optimize the allocation of the staff's time, arguably your most precious resource.
3. The study can be used for comparison with alternative processes.
4. It helps create target times and wage incentives.
5. You enhance efficiencies, staff time, and financial metrics.

Here are a half dozen tips for how to do a proper time study.

First, choose the appropriate tasks and processes to study. Be sure to include all aspects of the task/process to capture all time involved. You can do a time study on how you currently perform the task first. If you have an alternative approach to that task, you can do a time study on that second approach, and then compare the two.

Second, determine the number of cycles to study. At a minimum, design the time study to measure at least 2+ cycles to capture variances between different employees, occupancy rates, working conditions, times of year, etc.

Third, choose the appropriate staff to participate. Pick employees who are involved in the process. Include multiple staff as they may get different results, and such variances can be meaningful. Select the average staff members, not the fastest or slowest performers.

Fourth, explain the time study details to your team members. Communication is key for success. A time study requires careful observation, and you need staff to understand the details so that it does not disrupt their work or deliver inaccurate results. Reassure them why the time study is being done and cover any concerns they have about job security.

Fifth, have a manager/observer analyze individual tasks and results.

Finally, use data to calculate standard time and draw conclusions. Calculate the standard time between studies, then draw conclusions to improve efficiencies and optimize workflow.

Jennifer Wolf Pierson's team has also been very successful with time and cost savings. Her priority is focusing on her number one expense line item – which is payroll. As such, her teams do time studies for many of their processes to be sure they are spending their time on the area with the greatest return on investment, and to be certain that their activities will improve employee engagement and reduce turnover. This also means rewarding employees by paying more, as you get what you pay for these days.

Ben Day is also a big supporter of conducting time studies as a fact-based foundation for time and cost savings programs. He also recommends that as part of your cost savings programs you need to be sure to measure and compare not only where employees spend their time, but also where and how much they are using scarce resources such as water.

Jerrica Owen also has a lot of experience driving sustainability in terms of time and cost savings. She has had a lot of success in focusing on process improvements, by looking at all the steps involved in each process. As one example, at one animal shelter they determined that it was taking four hours to process an adoption and get the animal ready to go to their new home. This included steps which were paper based, where people needed to print out forms, fill them out, walk to printers and elsewhere, etc.

When the shelter switched to a cloud-based process, this not only saved lots of trees, but also reduced a lot of process time. They also worked to change the steps from a silo-based perspective where each person and/or department did things they thought were best from their perspective, but ignored how their steps interacted with others, instead taking a holistic approach from beginning to end. After doing all of this analysis they were successful in reducing the adoption process from four hours down to around one hour! The new cloud-based approach not only saved lots of time, but ended up with better cross-functional training and operations, as well as lower costs.

Having been privileged to see one of Jess Okon's great presentations on time studies at pet care conferences, we wanted to share some of her helpful insights regardless of what type of pet business you have. Especially if you are new to your business, you may not know where to start. Based on her experiences, she suggests starting by identifying the bottlenecks, which in other words are places where annoying traffic jams bring everything to a crawl, and foul up your efficiency.

Here are six common time-sucking tasks:

1. Check-In and Check-Out
2. Feeding and Medication,
3. Cleaning and Sanitation,
4. Leashing and Unleashing Dogs
5. Administrative Tasks/Client Communications
6. Bathing and Grooming

Once you've identified the area(s), you determine the goal, decide what tools you need, and determine the details. You can then work to streamline workflows, reduce wait times to boost customer satisfaction, and allocate resources effectively by using data-driven insights.

Alex Varney's plan for time and cost savings focuses mainly on reducing labor costs in their 10,000 square foot facility and consists of standardizing everything with Standard Operating Procedures (SOPs). They started with Time Studies, and built digital check lists to increase personal accountability for everyone involved in tasks such as cleaning, feeding, etc.

Some of the benefits included improved accuracy, reduced mistakes, and lower labor costs. This also helped improve their Enrichment in some creative ways. One of her favorite examples was transforming the enrichment shelf in the back of her facility, a place that everyone had to walk to and from every time they wanted an enrichment tool.

They replaced the shelf with an enrichment cart and moved it next to the sink so that as soon as enrichment tools were cleaned they could immediately be transferred to the cart. They then could wheel the cart around wherever it was needed, saving countless steps and time, which then transferred into more financial savings. This also raised the energy level of the staff, reduced errors, and made their jobs easier.

Matt Pepper at Michigan Humane shared some very interesting time study data with us. These studies pointed out that it cost Michigan Humane $680 to work to keep the dog in their pet parents' home, but that the cost escalated up to $1200 when the dogs entered the shelter, even before they had done much to help them. This indicated to them that they should focus on getting animals out of the shelter and at home, and when the animals must enter the shelter that they get them in and back out as fast as possible.

In terms of time and cost savings Eve Molzhon is a heavy user of time studies. As an example she shared a great one with us regarding folding laundry for boarding/daycare dogs. She and a colleague each measured how long it takes to fold a basket full of blankets, rags, and towels, and to put them away. Their result was 12 minutes.

As her facilities do 22 loads of laundry every day, this is a lot of time every day. She also asked her colleague what the dogs care about, and naturally they both agreed the dogs don't care if the blankets, rags, and towels are folded immaculately. So, they bought some Rubbermaid garbage cans, marked them on the outside as to what was inside each one i.e. clean rags, towels, sheets, etc. Then instead of carefully folding all this laundry they simply focused on tossing the clean laundry into the correct cans without folding.

After having done this, they discovered the amount of time involved went down from 12 minutes to just 6 minutes. When you multiply 6 minutes of time savings by 22 loads every day by 365 days per year by the hourly labor rate the time and money savings here are huge (803 hours a year!).

Is your facility design efficient and effective?

Dianna Starr's view on time and cost savings with wet/dry cleaning systems is fairly straightforward. By working with progressive architects and putting in the right cleaning systems you will not only reduce the time the staff spends cleaning, but also you will lower your utility bills.

Scott Learned also shared lots of cost savings opportunities which are sustainable in animal care buildings. For example, for a properly ventilated animal care building, energy recovery is a much better use of your money vs. insulation. As an example, he cited a 8,000 square foot facility with 30% fresh air, and he pointed out that fresh air costs as much as 83% of HVAC utilities. He said that tripling the insulation alone would only reduce costs by 11%, whereas installing energy recovery ventilators would reduce costs by 62%.

Scott also shared with us some of the pros and cons of different HVAC systems. Ground sourced heat pumps – which use the earth to absorb and reject heat – offer a very low operating cost. The con is they are very often undersized by the vendor as animal care has high fresh air loads and dehumidification requirements.

Ground water sourced heat pumps – which use well or pond water to absorb and reject heat – also offer low operating cost and require electricity for pumps, compressors, and are easy to install. The con is under sizing which is also a risk as many states limit heat injections into an aquifer. Cooling tubes – which use the earth to absorb and reject heat – offer low operating costs requiring only electricity for fans. The con is they are not a complete cooling and heating source.

Importantly, Energy Recovery ventilators offer 45% of summer and up to 65% winter effectiveness in transferring heat. Other pros include reduced utility costs and reduced HVAC equipment sizing. Some of the cons include more ductwork and some additional maintenance.

Some of the insights that Scott Learned shared with us related to trends in plumbing for animal care engineering include water saving fixtures and solar water heating. For water saving fixtures the pros include saved water, reduced drainage sizing, minimized chemical usage and more automated systems which are easier to use and require less labor.

There are not many cons, but in some cases cleaning systems have higher construction costs. With solar water heating the pros include that it is a mature technology, lower cost option in most cases vs photovoltaic options.

This approach can often provide 100% of an animal facility's hot water. Some of the cons include limited hot water generation on intermediate sunlight days, moderate construction costs, and that an adequate back-up water capability is still required. Scott also shared with us that non-pvc materials pros suggest that metal piping is stronger than PVC or PEX. The con to non-pvc can be the cost of installation and material, and metallic pipe may require water treatment to prevent corrosion.

Some of the challenges that Scott points out include that in the animal care world that leaders need to be more educated in the real cost and return on investment with buildings and chosen features. He points out that very few sustainable features are free, and many can cost quite a bit. He notes that a lot of architects and builders tell clients the return on investment for some features ranges from two to four years, whereas from Scott's calculations the real payback period is probably closer to 12-15 years given the significant amount of upfront money involved.

Very interesting to the author, Scott points out that typically animal shelters have more resources to invest in sustainability than boarding facilities and vet hospitals, as shelters raise money through donors to pay for the sustainability versus a boarding or vet facility needing to take out a loan.

Here are some of the electrical trends that Scott Learned wants to stress. Cogeneration is one trend – this consists of a generator where waste heat is consumed for space heating and water heating. The pro is that it is basically free heat. Some of the cons include high up-front cost, often excessive unused heat, and tough to balance.

With solar power the pro is free electricity, and the cons include high up-front costs, consuming a lot of roof area, and that rapidly improving technology can cause obsolescence. In terms of advanced lighting and controls the pros include good lighting and electricity controls with low consumption LED fixtures, photo sensitive controls, occupancy sensors, and remote web-based access.

The cons may include high upfront costs, particularly for LED lighting, and lighting benefit may be limited. In terms of lighting controls, the benefits include that they save money. Skylights and huge windows may not be so good – it depends among other things, upon the building siting and the geographical region in which the facility is operating.

Scott's sustainable design summary includes locally sourced exterior finishes, alternatives to PVC, better floor planning for circulation and isolation, energy recovery ventilation, high efficiency HVAC motors/compressors/burners/surfaces, reduced water consumption fixtures/cleaning systems, LED lighting, and daylighting in hallways / public / staff areas.

Given that the scope of this book is mainly to educate people in the pet boarding and animal shelters, there are opportunities to be successful, not only in the operations of the businesses, but very importantly in the design of the facilities in which these service businesses conduct most of their business.

Jess Okon's success stories with moving to automated metered dispensing systems for cleaning supplies saved them lots of time and money. She also has a lot of expertise in using time studies to save all types of pet facilities time and money. Her approaches are so effective that she is often invited to speak on this topic of time studies at some of the industry's best pet care conferences.

Part of the beauty of her approaches is their simplicity. She stresses that you can simply use a stopwatch and a piece of paper, in an exercise that will quickly show you how to save time, which is money.

With just a little more effort, she suggests you can also make videos with your phone for the time study, as this not only measures the exact process accurately, but also allows you to use the video for training other employees to do the process as effectively and efficiently as possible. This empowers you to spend less time on areas that are costing you money and enables you to spend more on enrichment and/or where you can make more money.

Mark Klaiman's experience has been that when a facility invests in initiatives to benefit the environment, most of the time these help that facility to make more money by saving even more money. For example, by switching from foaming guns to electrostatic sprayers, he has seen savings with fewer chemicals, less water usage, and lower power bills.

He says it is vital to have defined up front the Key Performance Indicators (KPIs) that measure and report on the investments, as well as their short-term outcomes.

Make technology your friend.

Dan Poirier points out that technology can do a great job achieving time and cost savings. This includes staff management systems, scheduling, shift swapping, and timekeeping.

This can all be automated now, which not only saves a lot of time, but also saves on paper which translates into material cost savings. Additional benefits for the staff include making things more flexible including getting their schedule on the phone, and/or change/swap without bothering management, and being more confident and autonomous in the process.

His team's PACKPRO staff training system product is fully automated to save lots of time, including systematically checking training boxes as the staff member works through the different sections of the training. This also has some benefits for enrichment programs. By automating so many processes, the staff ends up with more time to spend on enrichment. This applies not only to boarding, but also daycare, grooming and other services.

Eve's team also is a big believer in digital tools for achieving time and cost savings. After hours they use Voiceover IP to route callers to the right place. Eve also has 5 virtual assistants to help her run the businesses, including spending a fair amount of time on Facebook Market Places to find materials for the team to recycle and repurpose materials, thus saving money in the process. As 80% of her clients contact them between 6 PM and 11 PM, they use auto responses to save time, and to acknowledge and thank their clients.

Gary Weitzman and his administrative team are huge believers in using AI for time savings at the management level. Some uses include running meeting minutes through AI, using it for meeting summaries, and for putting together presentations. Gary said that for him alone AI saves several hours every day. Also, as he says, while we're all afraid of AI, it does let you get a lot more stuff done!

One highly effective—and often overlooked—tactic to supercharge Chapter 5: Achieving Time and Cost Savings is embracing full-featured pet care automation software. Businesses like Gingr, Kennel Connection, and MoeGo are designed to streamline the day-to-day by automating hosting, billing, scheduling, client communication, and even inventory tracking.

Gingr, for instance, reports efficiency gains by reducing time spent on repetitive tasks, opening up staff capacity for enrichment or mission-related work. Some facilities can reclaim as many as 10–20 hours a week from administrative relief, thanks to automated booking, reminders, and invoicing that not only cut labor cost but also improve client satisfaction.

By integrating such platforms, pet businesses see fewer errors, faster transactions, happier staff, and more time for what truly matters—animal enrichment and care—making it a seamless complement to your current time-study and SOP-driven strategies.

Other ideas to save time and money:

Regardless of what type of pet/animal care business you are in, time/cost savings must be part of your mindset. Many of you may have some sort of small retail area either onsite or online. Are you looking for solutions to make it more sustainable?

But you say, you haven't been able to figure it out so far? Well, here is a story from Charlotte Bigg's pet resort in Texas.

Their pet resort's retail area was time consuming, largely manually managed, and not delivering the cash flow needed to make it an ongoing part of the business. Some of the problems were caused by the staff pricing items at what their guts told them to, as opposed to checking costs, competitor pricing, and the actual margins. While today there are more sophisticated ways to handle these problems, back then Charlotte created an Excel spreadsheet, inserted the real product costs, and did some competitor price comparisons.

After explaining to the staff WHY they needed to do this and HOW it would benefit the employees as well, the staff bought in. The positive outcomes were numerous. First, it saved the staff time and helped with engagement. It also improved the margins so that the retail area became a real contributor to the business. Very importantly, it then also improved client satisfaction. Best of all, after seeing these benefits, it prompted the staff to use a similar new process to set up pricing for the new grooming service they launched.

Anna Radle's idea on achieving cost savings includes buying larger amounts, or formulas that go a lot further. For example, they used to buy broth to put on the dogs' food, and with up to 150 dogs per day they were buying huge amounts and having to deal with loads of excess packaging waste. So she switched to Boullion which is mixed with water. This allowed them to prepare much more food with less product, and a lot less waste, saving them lots of money as well.

Apryl Steele at Colorado Humane shared a distinct perspective on time and cost savings, one that we have heard from many other people in the industry. She says that partnering with a reliable, science-based nutrition partner in Hill's Nutrition has been a great relationship. She says that many shelters depend on donated pet food, which can vary significantly in terms of the type of food, ingredients, nutritional value, brand, etc.

Moreover, constant change in feed type can negatively impact animals' health. Apryl says that by working with Hills they receive consistent food supplies which significantly reduces investments in addressing intestinal issues, diarrhea flareups, cleaning, etc. Her team has measured and noticed significant cost savings vs. donated food, which can vary in quality. She also cites this consistent food supply is also a massive time saver for staff in not having to clean up after upset tummies.

Dom shared with us a different way to achieve time and cost savings for the for-profit side of pet care. He specifically recommends making your marketing sustainable. He suggests that you design your marketing content to allow it to be repurposed as often as possible, and to shift the work to clients when possible.

For example, he suggests asking your clients to do testimonial videos which direct prospects to your website where they are rewarded with a free, value-added gift like a tip sheet when they subscribe to your newsletter. This then can lead to automated follow-ups. As you can see, this creates a virtuous, circular, and sustainable set of marketing activities.

He believes that two of the biggest areas of sustainability for longevity are being premium priced and "niched down." He also believes in reducing waste, improving operational efficiencies, and building a business that lasts by being structured, profitable, and scalable. From Dom's perspective, some of the biggest challenges for the for-profit side of pet care include underpricing (which limits ability to invest in the business), not being profitable, burnout/high staff turnover, and competing on price vs. value.

Creating a local Pet Ministry also contributes in some surprising ways to helping local pet boarding/daycares and animal shelters, including to achieve more time and cost savings. Putting on a Blessing of the Animals event to help local Animal Care & Control organizations recruits more volunteers and donations, helps them tighten their focus on more productive activities-- including enrichment-- to do more for less, and empowers them to spend more time with the animals.

In terms of achieving more time and cost savings for for-profits that a Pet Ministry can assist, it is helpful to partner up with a local boarding/training facility with an animal shelter promotionally. For example, have the boarding facility offer a promotion to their pet parent clients that every time they purchase a treat for their pet while at their facility, the boarding facility will donate a free treat to an animal at the local shelters. In this way the Pet Ministry not only helps their community, but also saves for-profit and non-profit organizations money.

Top 10 Learnings from Chapter 5: Achieving Time and Cost Savings

1. Time Studies Drive Efficiency Across All Operations

Conducting time studies enables pet care businesses to identify inefficiencies, reduce wasted effort, and optimize workflows. This data-driven approach ensures staff time is focused on high-value tasks like enrichment or other revenue-generating services, leading to improved outcomes for animals, staff morale, and financial sustainability.

2. Automating Administrative Tasks Saves Time and Boosts Staff Satisfaction

Using platforms like Gingr, MoeGo, and Kennel Connection automates booking, invoicing, client communication, and scheduling. This reduces manual errors, cuts labor hours, and increases client satisfaction—all while freeing staff to focus on mission-critical tasks like pet care and enrichment.

3. Simple Process Redesigns Can Deliver Massive Time Savings

Eve Molzhon's laundry-folding time study cut 6 minutes per load across 22 daily loads by tossing clean laundry into labeled bins rather than folding. This kind of low-tech innovation multiplied over time produces huge cost savings and more time for enrichment or other high-value work.

4. Digital Checklists and SOPs Improve Accountability and Cut Labor Costs

Alex Varney's digitized SOPs and checklists led to reduced mistakes, streamlined operations, and lower labor costs. Her enrichment cart innovation, which saved staff countless steps per day, is a prime example of redesigning workflows to support sustainability.

5. Switching to Digital and Cloud-Based Systems Saves Time and Paper

Jerrica Owen's shift from paper-based to cloud-based adoption systems reduced the adoption process from 4 hours to 1 hour. This also improved cross-department collaboration and reduced printing and physical handling, directly supporting sustainability goals.

6. Sustainable Cleaning Systems Lower Utility Bills and Labor Costs

Investing in electrostatic sprayers, metered dispensing systems, and vacuum-based cleaning reduces water use, chemical waste, and cleaning time. Jess Okon and Jennifer Wolf Pierson both cite these approaches as major time and cost savers while improving animal and staff well-being.

7. Integrating Technology into Staff Management Increases Flexibility and Reduces Overhead

Systems that automate time tracking, shift swapping, and training—like PACKPRO—empower employees while reducing administrative overhead. These tools improve team efficiency and retention by creating a more autonomous, less stressful work environment.

8. Marketing Automation Creates Circular, Cost-Efficient Campaigns

Dom's approach to sustainable marketing—such as client-generated testimonials and automated follow-up workflows—lowers marketing labor costs while boosting engagement. These cycles improve ROI and brand loyalty with minimal time input.

9. Efficient Building and System Design Yields Long-Term Savings

Scott Learned and Eve Molzhon show how architectural and engineering innovations like centralized plumbing hubs, solar water heating, and energy recovery ventilation reduce utilities, construction complexity, and ongoing operational costs.

10. Consistent Nutrition Partnerships Reduce Cleaning and Health Costs

Apryl Steele's partnership with Hill's Nutrition reduced the frequency of digestive issues in shelter animals, lowering cleaning needs and associated labor costs. Standardizing nutrition can offer significant time and cost savings, especially for shelters dealing with donated, inconsistent food.

"You shouldn't try to change a system without the people who live in it."
—*Jerrica Owen*, Executive Director, National Animal Care & Control Association

Chapter 6: Integrating the 4 P's into Everyday Practices

The experts say:

Understanding the 4 P's of sustainability and how they will benefit your pet/animal care business is the all-important starting point. The next challenge is how to implement these into your business. This includes having a proactive plan to overcome challenges and resistance to change. Even after you've started that, you will need to have the right processes in place to monitor and measure success.

Are you in a place where you haven't yet started your business or you've been in business for years but are still not getting the sustainability results you believe you need? Are you frustrated because you've tried several things, but to no avail?

Well, based on what I've learned from so many successful pet pros, two areas in which you must invest include staff education and Standard Operating Procedures. In the case of Charlotte Biggs' pet resort in Texas, her emphasis was on teaching her staff the WHY the SOPs were the right approach so that she got their buy-in and support and avoided having them try too many other approaches that did not work.

As part of the preparation for such a plan, anticipate staff's objections, and be prepared with the WHYs. Also, for successful implementation of new processes, be aware of the true costs of implementation.

Another great piece of advice from so many veterans of pet/animal care with sustainable practices is to start small and scale up step by step. This can include steps like recycling, composting either locally or through services, saving energy, establishing SOPs for the core processes, and putting education plans in place for your staff.

Jerrica Owen's experience with integration usually involved starting small, and then scaling up. She said that pilot programs do this very well. She then uses ongoing learning to continue improving things. She also stressed that involving local businesses and getting champions within your teams to drive progress forward is very important.

These champions can not only get the pilot programs off the ground, but also can solicit input from various sources to learn about issues, figure out how to manage the issues, and overcome resistance to change. When doing this with KPIs, it keeps people moving forward. As they say, what gets measured gets done.

Several of the industry leaders that we interviewed stressed the importance of how to implement it correctly. They all stress that early on and on an ongoing basis, you should solicit staff input. Upfront input from your staff is particularly valuable as the staff are closest to the action, generally know what is really going on, and may also be the primary benefactors from their own input.

When asked about insights on how to better integrate sustainability practices into everyday practices, Apryl Steele's first response was to ask the staff, as the culture at Humane Colorado is to always ask and think how can we do better? Recently she asked a staff member for an improvement idea, and the staff member immediately said to change where they store things and put them right next to the place where they are used.

When this idea was implemented, the staff no longer had to walk half way across the facility to get what they needed. They then built on that by asking the staff to map out their day, and where they needed to go which yielded even more time savings and made them all more joyful!

Gary Weitzman shared a different perspective on how to get sustainability integrated into everyday practices. He emphasizes aspects of their culture of care and doing things that support their mission. Some specific tactics include making sure you remember everyone's names, making each person feel important, and when you see them ask them what they are proud of doing today before they go home.

Jess Okon has some similar views on implementation, including how to overcome fear or aversion to change. She stresses rallying the team, giving them a little time, and showing some patience. If after all that effort, there are still staff members who refuse to adopt or get on board with changes, perhaps that employee needs more scrutiny as to whether they are a sustainable part of the team or not?

Alex Varney's comments on integrating sustainability into everyday operations are all focused on education. She is adamant that being complacent is not sustainable, and you should never stop learning as the world, including your business, is always changing. In terms of resources to do this she points out all the great educational conferences there are to attend and learn from in many ways.

Anna Radle's team very often uses time studies to help them simplify complex problems into simpler solutions and to integrate them into everyday practices. The case study she cites from her own pet facility has to do with the movements of animals which involved lots of labor.

Due to some renovation work they were doing on their campus, they ended up hand walking dogs one by one outside and across the property. They calculated this was taking them about 45 minutes. So, while replanning how to map animal movements between enclosures, outside play areas, and nap areas, activities which staff performed multiple times per day, they switched from hand walking them to chuting the dogs carefully down a passageway with staff on each side leading them from one area to another, reducing the transit time from 45 minutes to just eight minutes.

Matt Pepper at Michigan Humane stresses KPIs like many others, and he takes it to the next level. He stresses that very often members of his community would say "so what?" when they cite KPIs, as they are not perceived to be relevant to the public. He stresses that KPIs should be designed so that they connect the animal shelter with the community's priorities.

As an example, there was a CEO of a Detroit area children's hospital who would not donate to the Michigan Humane as he said he and the hospital focused on human children, not animals. Matt responded by saying that 80% of dog bites in Detroit with kids were on their hands and face on their own property because the dog was unsocialized or medically not feeling well. The hospital CEO then said he would donate to Michigan Humane as he now understood that their work in the community with veterinary care and behavioral support was creating safer environments for children.

Another lesson here from Matt is to look at KPIs differently as an industry overall, highlighting how implementation of KPIs helps communities in more relevant ways. For example, a shelter shouldn't say "here's my live release rate" as many people in Detroit view that as only a number. Restating that statistic in a manner that highlights the positive impact to the community results in better reception. He shared two other stories of how to better connect with the community.

One, at their food pantry he asked a visiting lady if he could pet her dogs? This spurred a conversation in which she told Matt that she now depended on the food pantry for feeding her dogs as her parents and sister who had supported her earlier were now deceased, and how grateful she was for the support. Two, there was a woman on the east side of Detroit named Cynthia who had no legs and only one arm.

During COVID she got a wheelchair, and Michigan Humane helped her to get food for her cats, sterilized the cats, did all the vaccines, etc. This allowed her to keep her cats which otherwise would have had to have been re-homed, and this was what kept her going during a very hard time in life.

Dan Poirier is also big on finding systemic ways to integrate sustainability practices into everyday practices. For him, one of the biggest advantages is having a system to automate the onboarding process which brings a lot of benefits in terms of consistency in training and ongoing practices. As the goal is to produce a new star on your team in two weeks with training, they now have prepared digital new hire packets with everything compiled in advance, ensuring that the new hire packets are complete and thorough. There are also advantages to doing this on an ongoing basis, and his team now has the employee handbook stored electronically in DocuSign.

From Apryl's perspective there are many challenges facing sustainability in pet care today. Funding is a huge challenge as it keeps getting more expensive to hire staff to clean and feed animals, hire and engage a behavior team, an enrichment team, and good nutrition for all animals.

She stresses that they don't make money on adoption fees, and her adoption fees only cover about 15% of the costs. She stresses how important it is to engage their staff's work to be sure they value the work they are doing, and to get community buy-in. The stock market volatility changes donations, which is difficult as the number of animals with medical issues increases the number of veterinarians she must have as the medical and behavioral issues are growing.

Dianna Starr's view on integrating sustainability into everyday practices is to be sure you hire and listen to progressive people in design, construction of your building, and with your team to be sure you are buying the right cleaning equipment and have the right staff processes with the appropriate cleaning systems you have purchased. She has noticed huge changes over the past 20 years, and believes this continuous evolution is key moving forward.

Also, don't try to do it all yourself. In the pet resort world, you can find valuable resources at IBPSA (an industry non-profit association), Enrichment University, PackPro, The Dog Gurus, and others. In the animal shelter world, you can find great resources at NACA, Best Friends, Humane World for Animals (fka the Humane Society) and others.

Other ideas:

In terms of Pet Ministries helping to integrate sustainability into everyday practices, there are many examples across pet businesses. To start with, as more people and animals are feeling blessed, this enhances morale which improves progress with time, talent, and treasure.

With higher morale, overcoming challenges and resistance to change should be markedly improved. To help further turbocharge these benefits, engaging the community will result in better ideas, more buy-in, and naturally more sustainable results. As an example from Covenant's Pet Ministry, one of the team members who helps promote several of their services is also a volunteer at the local Animal Care & Control. She stepped up her support on Covenant's side while also building a stronger relationship with Animal Care & Control, and agreed to volunteer to help Covenant members who wanted to become more involved at AC&C by enabling them to shadow her during her duties.

Another complementary tactic comes from Natoo, a São Paulo-based pet brand accredited by the Pet Sustainability Coalition. Unlike one-off green initiatives, Natoo wove sustainability deeply into its core strategy—investing heavily in jaguar conservation, installing solar-powered manufacturing, and building biodiversity-themed in-store displays across 100 retail outlets (allpawsindustry.com).

This tactic enhances "integrating the 4☐P's into everyday practices" by transforming sustainability from an add-on into an intrinsic part of both product and place. It offers clear advantages: employees gain deeper purpose and engagement seeing real-world conservation impact, clients experience a meaningful brand story, and the business strengthens its planet positioning, yielding stronger loyalty and advocacy.

In short, Natoo's holistic approach shows that embedding environmental purpose into your business model uplifts people, planet, pet health, and profit simultaneously.

Top 10 Learnings from Chapter 6: Integrating the 4 P's into Everyday Practices

1. Educate Staff on the 'Why' Behind SOPs to Build Buy-In and Reduce Resistance

Teaching employees why Standard Operating Procedures (SOPs) matter creates alignment, minimizes deviation, and enhances implementation success. Charlotte Biggs' example underscores how upfront education leads to long-term consistency, better compliance, and stronger sustainability culture.

2. Use KPIs to Drive Impact and Connect with the Community

Matt Pepper emphasizes designing Key Performance Indicators (KPIs) that not only measure internal success but also resonate with community values. This alignment helps build public support, attract donations, and show how sustainability impacts broader human and animal welfare.

3. Start Small, Pilot, Then Scale Based on Feedback and Data

Veterans like Jerrica Owen recommend launching small-scale pilots and expanding based on what works. This reduces risk, boosts staff engagement, and supports continuous improvement. Piloting with measurable KPIs ensures data-driven decisions and sustainable growth.

4. Map Daily Workflows to Discover Simple, High-Impact Changes

Apryl Steele's team improved sustainability by mapping staff movement and reconfiguring supply storage. These simple changes saved time, improved morale, and eliminated wasteful practices. This shows how operational sustainability often starts with rethinking basic routines.

5. Create Internal Champions and Involve Staff in Decision-Making

Staff closest to the work offer the best insights for improving systems. Jerrica Owen and others emphasize giving staff ownership of changes to increase buy-in, drive innovation, and foster a collaborative sustainability culture.

6. Simplify Complex Challenges Through Time Studies

Anna Radle's time studies revealed that animal transit inefficiencies could be drastically reduced with chute-based movement. Time studies expose hidden inefficiencies and help embed sustainability into daily practices through streamlined operations.

7. Hire Progressive Teams and Use Modern Tools to Stay Ahead

Dianna Starr and Dan Poirier stress integrating sustainable practices through tech (like automated onboarding, cloud tools, and updated cleaning systems) and hiring staff aligned with progressive, sustainable values. This ensures long-term, systemic integration.

8. Never Stop Learning—Sustainability Is Constantly Evolving

Alex Varney advocates for attending industry conferences and staying curious. Ongoing education keeps your team up to date on innovations in animal care, environmental standards, and new business models—essential for long-term sustainability.

9. Connect Sustainability to Morale Through Pet Ministry and Community Engagement

Pet Ministries improve morale, attract volunteers, and increase collaboration between for-profit and nonprofit groups. These relationships create a culture of giving and shared purpose—making sustainable practices easier to implement and maintain.

10. Embed Sustainability into Core Strategy, Not Just Operations

Natoo's example of embedding sustainability into brand identity and retail operations shows how aligning all aspects of the business—product, purpose, and people—creates long-term environmental and financial gains.

A strategic approach to sustainability boosts loyalty, engagement, and impact. Also Gary Weitzman's focus on mission and making people feel important is a great way to integrate sustainability into core strategy and operations.

"The future of sustainability in pet care will be won by those willing to learn, adapt, and share what works."
— *Ben Day*, Pet Care Leader and Industry Consultant

Chapter 7: The Future of Sustainability in Pet Care

The future is both exciting and scary. Here are ideas on how to harness the energy of the future for a more sustainable world.

Embracing Artificial Intelligence:

Charlotte Biggs believes the future of pet care is very bright! Every year there are more and more tools to help move the industry forward. An important priority for all should be improving and getting ongoing help to optimize your SOPs.

Very importantly, and as the opportunity of a lifetime, she stresses that AI is going to help in many ways, and now is the time to jump on it. Even if you are intimidated by AI, you should start learning about it and how to use it now and, if it helps, start small.

Several of the pros we interviewed are big fans of AI and say it is already powerful and will only grow in importance. Ben Day emphasizes the industry's need to adapt to AI to be on the cusp of innovation and in the center of the future of the industry. He also mentions the need for the industry to change its mindset about sharing resources and knowledge to effectively integrate AI, indicating a necessary shift in culture and practices.

Ben also shared some of his experience with media inquiries regarding the industry's role in preventing catastrophic incidents, showcasing his expertise, and the industry's responsibility in addressing legislative concerns.

Jerrica Owen's perspective on the future of sustainability is optimistic and centers on how technology is going to continue to improve outcomes for animal care businesses. This includes a lot of AI, including programs such as PetCo's Love Lost facial recognition platform that has already been so helpful in the industry in reuniting animals with their pet parent families.

She also is excited about DocuPet's GPS health monitor tracker which includes measuring sleep scores, and jokes that the pets using this are getting better care than she does in some ways. She is also hopeful that future legislation and grants for renewable energy will be very beneficial. If you want to learn more about her organization and check out NACA, see https://www.nacanet.org/.

In terms of the future, Alex Varney focuses on increasingly using AI to reduce management time on projects, improving policy creation, and in some areas reducing labor time. She is also excited by biodegradable products such as waste bags. As there is virtually no legislation in Ohio regulating pet care, she is hopeful that in the future there will be help in the form of new legislation to assist with sustainability.

In addition to education, Anna Radel's other area of interest for the future is AI. She recently discovered that she could take three years of check lists, training materials, etc. throw it into AI and ask it to make her an eight-day training program, which it did instantly, and she loved it.

This will not only save her time, but it will also improve her operations and sustainability in countless ways. She also believes that education will continue to be a key success factor for the future and, when combined with attending conferences and networking, will keep you up to speed in the industry.

When asked about the future of pet care, Apryl Steele cited many important improvements on the horizon. For starters, she sees using AI to reduce data entry work and linking various tags on animals that track things to save even more data entry work. She says all leaders are dealing with more challenges with financial sustainability.

To help in this area, Apryl suggested that for those who reach out to donors who have been focusing on human investments to try to convince them to invest in the human-animal relationship. Emphasizing how much more of a return those new investments can bring while bringing even more benefits to humans in many areas including substance abuse is one great approach.

In terms of the future, Dan Poirier is also excited about what AI is already doing and will do going forward. In particular, with phone services he is excited about software that answers the phone, books appointments, updates vaccines, and redirects clients to other areas. In terms of the environment, he sees pet facilities finding more and more ways to use less water and, where appropriate, switching to foaming sprays.

Audrey's Barkyard in Wake Forest, NC, elevated their sanitation protocols by integrating **UV-C germicidal technology**—installing hospital-grade UV-C fixtures in vents and upper-room units throughout the facility□hpac.com+1petboardinganddaycare.com+1.

This proactive approach to airborne pathogen control complements Chapter 7's emphasis on AI and automation by adding a powerful physical layer of defense: the UV-C system continuously neutralizes microbes in the air and HVAC systems, improving animal health, reducing illness-related downtime, and lowering chemical and labor costs.

Compared to traditional cleaning, these fixtures add near-hands-free protection, extend equipment life, and align perfectly with the future-forward integration of robotic disinfection (like "Trudy") already being adopted by veterinary hospitals (stories.tamu.edu.) It represents a smart, scalable leap toward truly sustainable and high-tech environments in pet care.

As AI continues to come on board in the pet world, this will help all types of pet businesses not only to conduct business better, but also to staff appropriately and to track sustainability.

Don't forget technology.

Mark Klaiman is also optimistic about the future of pet care. He believes that we have already made a lot of progress with technology, and we will need new technologies to keep us moving forward. In the area of technology, there are already many things that you can use to help make you more sustainable. This includes using QR codes, new scanners, etc. to avoid printing out so many materials.

As most of the readers of this book are small businesses, Mark encourages all of us to learn from big companies when it comes to technology. Especially while small businesses have more financial flexibility than private equity owners who have other shareholders to take care of. He is also optimistic about ongoing progress from construction materials.

Another insight on the potential future of pet care sustainability from our author is based on his travels to France and Germany in spring 2024. At one restaurant they visited, they noticed that the restaurant used robots to gather dirty dishes from the customers' tables.

The robots then carried all these dishes to the kitchen area for washing. We asked about robots, and we were told they were used to reduce the labor time employees spent on low value work. We immediately thought that this could be something in the future for pet care facilities in the US.

Education and Leadership are the keys.

Anna Radle's view on the future of sustainability in pet care is all about education and focusing on learning more about dogs. She points out how much we have learned about dogs' body language and identifying what is going on versus twenty years ago. She believes we need to learn to be even more observant, and to try and test new things with dogs.

For example, if a dog is not resting well in her facility, that probably means that the dog has too much anxiety. If after trying many solutions the dog is still anxious, she may decide that her team may not be the best facility for that particular dog, as she says that unhappy dogs have a trickle down impact on other dogs and staff.

When that happens, Anna says it is very important to be proactively transparent with the pet parents that their dog does not belong at her facility. In other words, she won't take dogs who can't be happy and healthy with her team. She says we all need to learn more in this and related areas.

Dianna Starr believes that an important part of the future of pet care, both for non-profits and for-profits, involves the exhibitors/vendors who support educational conferences banding together so that attendees can learn of the proven vendors and work with them together as a team. These same vendor partnerships will also be important for the growing number of online conferences.

Matt Pepper also believes that we need to develop better leaders for industry and find ways to encourage them to stay longer. He notes that too many of them get inadvertently caught up in our cancel culture on social media, resulting in chasing away some of our best future leaders.

He is also in favor of having social workers who work alongside veterinarians who are better equipped to deal with people's problems, while vets focus on the animals, which is key for sustainability. In terms of technology, Matt believes that a lot of people in the industry are working on telehealth to expand access to services and reduce costs on the distribution model of resources. Matt also sees AI changing call centers as many of the shelter calls could possibly be handled by AI.

Dan Porrier also believes mental sustainability is not talked about enough today and should be a bigger topic going forward. For leadership and owners, running a pet facility is a challenging job, often including managing many living beings, both two and four legged.

For example, his two facilities have up to 60 employees as well as 60 dogs per day, all contributing to lots of stress and mental health issues. Dan believes we should be working more on helping leaders to manage their emotions, making sure they have systems in place, and other resources to set leadership up for success. As he points out, mental stability can make or break operations. When managed well, mental sustainability is a competitive advantage which helps management to focus on the longevity of the business using all possible means.

In terms of his definition of sustainability, Dan says it is building a business model that supports long-term success, with a strong focus on achieving better outcomes for dogs, the staff, the business, and the owners' interests. He says he runs into lots of newbies in the industry who get in and find out it is too hard and try to find a way to sell within 3 years given burnout, which often doesn't work out.

He says some of the biggest challenges include that boarding facilities are people-dependent businesses, and very often are running without true, sustainable systems and therefore rely too much on gut feel and daily heroics and are not set up for long term success.

Eve Molzhon is researching some potential innovative ideas for the future of pet care, including two new possibilities of what to do with dog poop. She is collaborating with a "poop-pumping" business guy to test the acidity of dog poop and to see how easy it might be to mix it with other organic products to make it a viable fertilizer. Another potential option she is researching is whether dog poop could help to break down part of the garbage we put in landfills.

As of the spring of 2025, she has done some research going to see how effectively dog poop will help break down retail shopping bags from Target, Walmart, and Menards, using sandy soil, brown neutral soil, and deep dark rich soil. So far, only one person has paid Eve for her business' poop, and that was a worm farmer who was going to make it into mulch.

Nevertheless, she persists in her belief that the idea will resonate sometime in the future. Other areas of interest for the future for Eve include doing more research on how water treatment could expand the longevity of pets. She is also investing over $10,000 each year in sending her staff to pet care conferences to learn more about potential ideas for the future, and to learn from the many questions she, and they, can ask at these events. She also advises people in the pet care industry to connect with Facebook groups, especially those focused on enrichment and holistic veterinarians.

Community and legislation.

Matt Pepper of Michigan Humane shared many of his insights on what the future of sustainability needs to move us forward. His first point is to place animal care industry leaders in a different light for the community, being seen as true partners, not just a necessity off to the side that is required for a municipality. He also believes we need to build a community of advocates as today there is a lot of confusion with brands and messages.

He believes this confusion merits industry consolidation to get to consistency across facilities. For example, in Detroit they have a large shelter, Detroit Animal Care & Control, and Michigan Anti-Cruelty Society, all of which have brick and mortar shelters. So, if your dog goes missing you don't know which one of these facilities picked up your dog, and you don't know how to find it.

He also believes these different facilities need to be restructured and to work together instead of experiencing infighting. To him, this means building a community based on consolidation to ensure consistency. He cites the examples of San Diego as well as Wisconsin Humane which now has five organizations on the eastern side of Wisconsin. Once things are consolidated, you find out who does the best job at different tasks, and you put the money where it is going to have the most positive impact.

Gary Weitzman's focus on the future of sustainability in animal care is on supporting legislation that supports their mission. He says that they are supporting 5 bills in California to make it almost impossible to run a puppy mill in certain situations. They are also trying to help legislation to make veterinary care more affordable.

The author visited Istanbul, Turkey in 2024, where he was positively amazed to encounter many healthy, happy, well-behaved and sociable dogs and cats in public places. He believes that a much better future could exist in the US if we adopted many of the sustainable initiatives that are already being used in Turkey today for "stray" animals.

Here is an overview of some of these sustainability initiatives. In Istanbul, Turkey, local authorities and communities have implemented several eco-friendly and efficient strategies to care for stray dogs and cats, aiming to ensure their well-being while minimizing the time and resources required from those involved.

Trap-Neuter-Return (TNR) Programs are one tactic. Istanbul employs TNR programs, where stray animals are humanely captured, sterilized, vaccinated, and then returned to their original locations with a tag identifying the animal. This method helps control the stray population over time without resorting to euthanasia. It also reduces behaviors associated with mating, such as aggression and roaming, making the animals less likely to cause disturbances. (source winssolutions)

They also use Eco-Friendly Feeding Initiatives. Innovative vending machines, known as "mamamatiks," have been installed throughout Istanbul and other large Turkish cities. These machines dispense food and water for stray animals when people deposit recyclable plastic bottles. This initiative not only provides sustenance for strays but also promotes recycling among residents, integrating environmental consciousness with animal welfare. (source daily Sabah)

Community Engagement and Shelter Support is involved in Istanbul. Local volunteers and animal lovers play a significant role by feeding, sheltering, and providing medical care for stray animals. Some individuals have established private shelters, offering safe havens for numerous strays. These community-driven efforts alleviate the burden on municipal resources and foster a culture of compassion. (Source Earthvagabonds)

Legislative Measures and Public Education also play a role in Turkey's Animal Protection Law, which mandates the humane treatment of stray animals, including their sterilization and vaccination. Municipalities are responsible for implementing these measures, and public education campaigns have been launched to raise awareness about responsible pet ownership and the importance of not abandoning animals. (Sources Vox and Winssolutions)

Regarding the future for sustainability in animal care, Scott Learned has shared many helpful insights. One he hopes for is that there will be more helpful future legislation focused on animal care facilities, as there is virtually nothing today compared to buildings for humans. He sees a big future for animal products with biodegradable properties, including cat litter boxes, which is a big unmet need at animal shelters nationwide today.

He is also very excited about photovoltaic roof shingles which he believes will significantly lower costs. He is looking forward to a brighter future with indoor air treatment with system improvements to mitigate odor and disease. Combining this with recirculating systems will also save lots of energy.

Thoughts from other resources.

Jess Okon gave a great example of the future of sustainability in terms of sustainable products. She cited Benebone's nylon bones, which give you information on how to return them for proper recycling after the dog has finished chewing them. This is yet another example that the future of sustainability is already here today in many cases.

Dom's view on the future of sustainability is clever and very useful. He notes that when you plan your business around premium pricing and a niche positioning you are setting yourself up today to generate the funds now to fund the investment for the future. This allows you the flexibility to build solid enrichment programs both for pets and people, and to invest in the areas of sustainability you find most compelling.

Texas A&M's Veterinary Medical Teaching Hospital utilizes a stationary robot named Tru-D (or "Trudy") for disinfection purposes. Trudy employs ultraviolet C (UVC) light to eliminate even the most resistant infection-causing bacteria on surfaces like walls, floors, and tables. This enhances sanitation, reduces infection risks, and minimizes the need for chemical disinfectants, thereby improving environmental sustainability and reducing labor demands. (sources Texas A&M VMBS and Tech Xplore).

To those of you interested in a view to the sustainable future in terms of protecting the earth, AMP Robotics based in the USA offers more than one solution today that could benefit the pet industries from a sustainability perspective (source Transformative Marketing by V Kumar and P Kotler). For example, AMP Cortex high-speed robotics system automates the sorting and identification of recyclables from mixed material streams.

It does this by recognizing, differentiating, and recovering recyclables based on attributes such as color, size, shape, opacity, and more. This sorting technology can select more than 80 items per minute, which is twice the speed of humans.

Building a Pet Ministry with a local network of sustainable pet care advocates through canine therapy with schools and/or homeless, and/or Blessing of the Animals will play a key role in this. In all these cases, canine therapy is helping humans to move forward with treatments which are effective and free and/or affordable. This can continue to build more sustainable relationships between a growing number of people and pets.

This will empower humans on the spectrum or stressed-out university students to do better academically, help homeless to get back on their feet with their lives, and strengthen the bonds of community members. They will continue to source their pets from animal shelters and/or send their pets to pet boarding facilities to lodge them including socialization benefits.

Top 10 Learnings from Chapter 7: The Future of Sustainability in Pet Care

1. Embrace AI to Improve Efficiency, Reduce Labor, and Enhance Sustainability

Across the industry, leaders like Charlotte Biggs, Ben Day, and Anna Radle emphasize the transformative role of AI—from creating instant training programs to automating admin tasks. AI improves operational efficiency; cuts waste and reallocates human effort to higher-value enrichment and care activities.

2. Implement Automated and Robotic Technologies to Reduce Labor and Improve Sanitation

Robotic disinfection (e.g., Tru-D), automated phone systems, and sanitation-enhancing UV-C systems (as used by Audrey's Barkyard) reduce labor costs, improve hygiene, and extend equipment life—all while supporting sustainability and staff health.

3. Design Businesses Around Premium, Niche Models to Fund Sustainability

Dom advocates building sustainable futures by charging premium prices tied to enrichment-focused services. This generates the revenue needed to invest in green tech, education, and long-term improvements while differentiating your brand.

4. Use Legislative and Grant Opportunities to Boost Renewable Energy Adoption

Jerrica Owen and Scott Learned highlight the future potential of grants and public policy to drive investments in clean energy like photovoltaic shingles and energy-efficient building systems—cutting emissions and utility costs for pet care facilities. For larger facilities like Gary's that have the resources to support state legislation to improve mission accomplishment should explore these options.

5. Align KPIs and Messaging with Broader Community and Human Benefits

Matt Pepper emphasizes that sustainability KPIs must resonate with external audiences. By linking pet welfare to human outcomes (e.g., dog bite prevention), organizations can gain support from donors and government entities, expanding their reach and impact.

6. Invest in Education and Conferences to Stay Ahead of Change

Veterans like Anna Radle and Eve Molzhon recommend continuous education to remain competitive and adaptive. Conference attendance, network learning, and Facebook groups help staff stay informed on emerging sustainability trends and tools.

7. Promote Mental Sustainability for Leadership and Staff

Dan Poirier stresses that sustainable operations depend on mentally resilient leadership. Supporting leaders with systems and emotional tools reduces burnout and ensures the long-term stability of pet care operations.

8. Adopt International Models for Scalable Sustainability Practices

Insights from Istanbul's TNR programs and eco-friendly vending machines ("mamamatiks") demonstrate low-cost, high-impact sustainability models. U.S. pet care operations can replicate these to reduce strays, promote recycling, and foster community compassion.

9. Foster Consolidation and Community Collaboration for Shared Impact

Matt Pepper recommends consolidating local shelters and animal care organizations to streamline operations, avoid duplication, and focus resources. Consolidation allows for specialization, clearer communication, and stronger donor engagement.

10. Innovate Through Sustainable Product Design and Recycling Systems

Examples like Benebone's recyclable nylon bones and AMP Robotics' AI-powered sorting machine shows that product and waste innovations are key to reducing landfill loads and improving brand reputation. These tools drive efficiency and sustainability across the product lifecycle.

Chapter 8 Conclusion

Adopting a sustainable strategy in pet / animal care is not just an option, it's the most powerful step forward for creating a thriving future for pets, people, businesses, and the planet. When guided by a proactive plan rooted in the 4 P's—Pets, People, Planet, and Profits—sustainability becomes a dynamic, purpose-driven force that elevates every aspect of a pet care operation.

A Proactive Plan Built on the 4 P's

1. Pets benefit from sustainability through better health, enriched environments, reduced stress, and more personalized care. Thoughtful facility design, high-quality food and water, structured enrichment, and behavior-sensitive programming (like the P.E.T. model) all contribute to happier, healthier animals. Cleanliness, air quality, and noise reduction strategies further enhance their daily experiences, reducing illness and behavioral issues.

2. People—from staff to pet parents—experience transformative outcomes through sustainable practices. Staff enjoy better training, higher wages, reduced burnout, and more autonomy, which leads to improved morale and lower turnover. Community engagement, education-first cultures, and emotional support deepen connection and create a culture

where employees thrive, and pet parents feel proud to participate.

3. Planet-friendly practices such as rainwater harvesting, automated chemical dispensers, solar panels, green transportation, and recycled materials dramatically reduce environmental impact. By designing operations around energy and water efficiency from the beginning, facilities can achieve lower utility bills, healthier environments, and long-term resilience. Even landscaping with bioswales and rain gardens can enhance biodiversity and mitigate flooding.

4. Cash Flow and Cost Savings/Profits become more consistent and sustainable through efficiency gains, strategic investments, premium pricing, and process automation. Time studies, cloud-based SOPs, and smart scheduling systems free up resources, reduce waste, and optimize workflows. This allows facilities to reinvest in innovations, staff development, and enrichment programs, creating a virtuous cycle of financial and operational growth.

The Outcomes: What Sustainability Delivers

Embracing a sustainable strategy redefines success in pet care:

Operational Excellence: Streamlined workflows, smarter cleaning systems, and modern technologies boost staff productivity, reduce mistakes, and improve animal outcomes.

Financial Resilience: Lower labor and utility costs, increased revenue through premium services, and greater staff retention mean more capital available to innovate and expand.

Enhanced Animal Welfare: Enrichment programs, better nutrition, stress-reducing facility features, and thoughtful kennel designs lead to healthier, more adoptable animals.

Stronger Community Connections: Engaging volunteers, spiritual programs like pet ministries, and community partnerships build support systems that increase visibility and sustainability. Additionally, a happier staff is stronger, more engaged with the community, and less likely to experience rapid turnover.

Future-Readiness: AI, technology, robotics, and legislative alignment prepare pet care operations to thrive in a rapidly evolving world, ensuring ongoing relevance and competitive advantage.

A Movement Worth Joining

Sustainability is not a trend, it's a movement. One built on long-term thinking, shared purpose, and the belief that we can care better—for pets, for each other, for our communities, and for the Earth. Whether you're just beginning or already well on your way, there's room to grow, innovate, and make a lasting impact.

Start small if you need to. Pilot new ideas. Involve your team. Educate your clients. Measure what matters. And above all, commit to the journey.

Now is the time to join the movement toward a greener, smarter, more compassionate future for pet care. Together, we can build facilities that nurture animals, empower staff, delight clients, and safeguard the planet—one sustainable choice at a time.

Chapter 9: Meet the Experts

If you are wondering about the author of the book, why he wrote this book, and why you should care, here is some information: Over the past 30+ years Alex McKinnon has leveraged his innovation expertise to solve increasingly complex problems in business.

His BA at Duke University and MBA from Northwestern's Kellogg School were a solid foundation. His formative years in Design, Innovation and Marketing in Spain were at Sara Lee and then at Braun. 10 more years at Braun included roles of increasing global responsibility in Germany, Scandinavia, and USA, achieving record growth in the health and oral care businesses, for humans.

Running Gillette's USA toiletries business broadened his consumable products expertise, and gave him lots of experience in grooming. His subsequent leadership roles at Bell Sports, Sylvan Learning, and Hampton Products gave him invaluable middle market and private equity exposure and success, which has been helpful as more private investors enter the pet boarding business.

The last 12 years have been exceptionally rewarding as Alex conceived, founded, and launched the award-winning Kinn brand of pet care products across B2B and B2C channels. Kinn has a strong focus on pet boarding facilities and animal shelters, helping pet facilities in all 50 states to improve their sustainability by adopting Kinns processes to improve outcomes for animals, staff, the planet, and progress/cost savings.

Alex has also learned that sustainability is foundational in pet care success. It is one of his key values. On a personal level, this means solar power on his last three homes, home recycling and composting programs, an electric vehicle, and of course sustainable products for their two third-chance rescue dogs Skye and Erin. In the pet care business, he became a member of the Pet Sustainability Coalition over ten years ago, and Kinn has been ranked in the top levels of sustainability in both environmental and societal areas over the years.

He decided to write this book when it dawned on him that there is no existing guide to sustainability for pet boarding facilities or animal shelters. As he wants to help many more pet pros, he decided to launch this book.

In 2023 he put together an educational program on Storytelling for the Professional Directors Association. It got such a positive response, he concluded that writing this sustainability book using stories would have the most impact. The vast majority of the stories in this book are based on relationships and/or interviews Alex has had with leaders across the country in animal shelters and pet boarding facilities.

Other Industry experts and contributors

Mark Klaiman, who is the founder and owner of the pet resort Pet Camp in San Francisco is also married to Virginia Donohue who works for San Francisco Animal Care and Control. Given this couple's cross channel perspective, we wanted to share some of their views on sustainability topics that show even more similarities between business types. The barrier to education, where people fail to stop and think about sustainability can be a big issue.

A lack of proper financial insights about costs of implementation and cash flow can be problematic. Some basic things that can be done to help both at the design stage, and operationally later on, include being very careful on what type of buildings to choose for the facility, buying commercial versions of washers, monitoring the spend in utilities, and something as basic as sweeping vs. using a hose.

In terms of understanding sustainability in animal care, one of the smartest and most analytical leaders that the author knows in the animal shelter world is Dr. Josh A. Fisher, MHA, CAWA, the Director of Animal Care & Control at Charlotte Mecklenburg in North Carolina. He has over 20 years of experience in the field, and 10 years in Charlotte where he has led his team's initiatives, which have almost doubled the success rate of finding homes for animals under their care.

Some of his priorities include efficient resource management, community engagement, the empowerment of staff to improve processes, and animal enrichment to grow adoption rates. Given his team's success, we delve into more details in several of the chapters of this book.

Jennifer Wolf-Pierson is the General Manager of ABC Pet Resort in Houston, Texas. In addition to this role, she is also a leader of Pet Care Bootcamp, involved in Turnkey, Inc., a designer of animal facilities, as well as a pet care industry thought leader / conference speaker. She has many great views on sustainability in pet care.

Another industry veteran who has extensive experience with sustainability is Ben Day who retired at the end of 2024 as the Chief Operating Officer of International Boarding and Pet Services Association (IBPSA). A lot of his experience is in CPR training and safety consulting, including a focus on social responsibility and support for vulnerable groups. Ben is also a big believer in education to foster excellence and ongoing improvement, and he points out that sustained investment in education is necessary to avoid the risk of becoming subpar.

Jerrica Owen at the National Animal Care & Control Association also brings a great deal of perspective as to what sustainability means in pet care. She started out at a small shelter which over the years grew to be one of the largest, and now brings in around 50,000 animals per year, enabling her to understand businesses of many sizes. Jerrica views sustainability as creating long term solutions for animals, people, and the environment.

She views some of the key success factors to involve training programs for staff, having the right equipment, and community access, all of which need to be data driven. Her experience shows that when you have these resources and outcomes you are best equipped to overcome the biggest challenges in animal shelters which include lack of resources/funding, staff burnout, and reuniting lost pets.

Jess Okon also has extensive operating experience focusing on sustainability in boarding/daycare facilities and training businesses. She has operated as a trainer and run pet boarding operations.

Dom Hodgson is an expert at understanding sustainability in pet care on the for-profit side, and runs a global consultancy and coaching company for pet care professionals out of the UK which also has a big following in the USA. He started his own "dog adventure" company in 2011 rather than a simple dog walking business, then grew into writing pet books / being a conference speaker. In 2016 Dom began helping clients with coaching in marketing and enrichment, and then launched Enrich University in 2017.

One of the people I have met who has a great understanding of sustainability in dog boarding, daycare, and training from the operational perspective is Alex Varney who runs Pinnacle Pets in Ohio. Pinnacle has been in business about eight years and has made so much progress, that now they also offer pro bono consulting to help others in the industry.

Alex totally understands that education is key in this day and age, and things continue to change all the time. She also has a keen understanding of the complexity of sustainability and that it is key to balance protecting the environment with the welfare of pets, people, and financial resources. She also has a lot of experience creating solutions for the industry's biggest challenges, including pet overcrowding, stress, and illness, as well as staff burnout, and turnover.

Anna Radle, after 21+ years running her own boarding facility and being a coach/consultant for The Dog Gurus has a firm grasp on what sustainability in pet care really means, especially on the for-profit side. In 2003 she bought an existing business, and has been growing and innovating for 21 years. She defines sustainability in pet care as staying in business, and thriving.

The foundation is ongoing education, consistent improvement, knowing that the industry is going to go through cyclical ups and downs, living within your means, and much more. She focuses on empowering and educating clients to keep ahead of her competitors which she defines as the "girl next door." This requires her to differentiate her offerings, and use enrichment to always deliver a superior experience for the pets.

With over 25 years of experience in pet care helping clients with wet/dry cleaning systems, Dianna Starr brings a lot of understanding to the table in understanding sustainability in pet care. She partners with pet business owners in for-profit and non-profit, as well as the space designers, architects and builders. One of the biggest challenges she sees fairly often is old school thinking about building design. She sees architects still insisting on expensive drain networks which can cause many problems including high water bills, high drain demands, buildings not being clean, more outbreaks and illnesses for pets and staff, and higher costs.

Scott Learned brings a unique and valuable perspective to sustainability in pet care with his expertise in designing and building animal care facilities. Thirty years ago he received his professional engineering degree. One of his first jobs was designing jet engines, but he quit this job and opened his own consulting firm focusing on designing boarding facilities.

He then got into designing vet hospitals and animal shelters. He also began to lecture at ABKA educational conferences (name changed to Pet Care

Services Association in 2008). His firm continued to evolve as more and more architects asked him for advice. He now has a fully staffed firm with architecture, interior design, engineering, program management, etc. exclusively focused on animal care. As a LEED (Leadership in Energy and Environmental Design, a globally recognized green building rating system) accredited professional – which is earned by passing the LEED exam administered by Green Business Certification Inc.-- his expertise is sought after as animal facilities very often need very different things than buildings for humans. Knowledge helps them avoid incorrectly designing and building their new facilities, and results in the optimal space for the most important animal needs.

Scott was also kind enough to share his insights as to what are the sustainable trends in animal facility buildings in terms of design features, including the following. First is better floor planning which promotes circulation and better isolation. Second is extensive use of high efficiency windows.

Daylighting – the use of natural light to illuminate spaces -- with clerestory windows – a row of windows placed high on a wall above eye level to bring natural light in--, and resin based finishes and flooring particularly in lieu of PVC products. Lastly, local sourced materials, particularly structural materials such as steel and masonry, and exterior finishes.

Brad Shear, as CEO of Potter League of Animals in Middletown RI, started his career in animal shelters in Boulder, CO and has had an interest in sustainability from the beginning. He and the author also share mutual enthusiasm for the Pet Sustainability Coalition (PSC) in Boulder, where the author and his company Kinn have been members for over 10 years.

Matt Pepper of Michigan Humane has an extensive knowledge of understanding sustainability in pet care. His definition of sustainability is the ability to provide services in their community, and ensuring they are all affordable, accessible, and reachable with transportation. For animal shelters he says there are multiple key challenges starting with uncertainty in philanthropy. To serve his particular community they need to raise $23 - $24 million every year, and as of 2025 the uncertainty around the economy is making it hard to plan accordingly.

This money will only enable them to serve the existing 12,000 families, including 2.3 million pounds of pet food, and does not leave much money to grow. When you combine the fast growth in the cost of veterinary staff / care, it makes balancing the budget even harder.

Apryl Steele, as CEO of Humane Colorado, with 20 years prior experience as a Veterinarian has rich experience and understanding of sustainability in pet care. Importantly, her perspective on sustainability in animal care with animal shelters has developed, as when she started as CEO, the work was 90% housing and caring for animals and has now evolved to 50% housing and caring for animals and 50% helping to keep animals in their families.

The foundation of this work now also includes getting animals out of the shelter as fast as possible. While the animals are at the shelter, the shelter owns the animals in care, making medical and behavioral care priorities. Improvements in these areas makes animals less stressed and anxious, making them happier and thus resulting in better outcomes and adoptions.

Apryl's team describes their philosophy as socially conscious, where they want to be a safe place for every animal that needs them regardless of health, age, and adoptability. They focus on a lot of the length of stay metrics as the average cost of caring for an animal at their facility has grown from $440 to $800 over the past five years.

Given they have 20,000 animals come in every year, the costs are growing rapidly. That being said, their stated mission is to impact homelessness and animal suffering. To make this sustainable and to reduce the length of stay, they focus on providing animals walks and hikes, as well as enrichment. This helps to avoid anxious / stressed animals and allows them to display better behavior to improve adoptions. Apryl also delicately shared with us her wisdom on the difficult topic of euthanasia. If despite her high-quality team's best efforts with medicine and behavioral care combined with enrichment the dog still persists in showing really vicious, dangerous behavior, most often the pet should be euthanized rather than keeping a dangerous, miserable animal by itself in a kennel by itself for years on end. This also frees up resources to help save many other animals.

Dan Poirier, as co-founder/owner of both daycare/boarding facilities and online staff training company PACKPRO, brings a rich perspective on the sustainability in pet care, and has been focused on this since opening in 2012 with his cousin and business partner Mal Poirier. Dan says when they launched Fetch n' Catch their mindset was this was going to be their career, and they were focused on how to make the business make sense for the long term. Soon after launching, they realized they were in over their heads and decided to double down on the long term, and to focus on the next 10 years, with specific initiatives for the dogs, the staff, and the dollars coming in to support them.

Their approach seems to have worked very well as they are now the largest daycare/boarding facility in the Buffalo, NY area. Dan said they made lots of mistakes along the way, but importantly kept learning from these issues. In 2018 they felt they had learned enough to make a separate business to help others in the industry to avoid making their mistakes when they soft launched PACKPRO online staff training program, and they did a hard launch in 2020 as they had to shut down Fetch n' Catch for a short period due to Covid.

After twelve years in pet care, Eve Molzhon definitely has a strong understanding of the power of sustainability in the industry. In this book we share some of the stories of how she started as we believe there are some good lessons for many of us.

Gary Weitzman has spent decades in animal care as a Veterinarian and senior executive in animal welfare, and currently he is President of San Diego Humane Society, one of the country's largest animal welfare non-profit organizations. His understanding of sustainability in animal care is extensive, and filled with realism and dreams.

When asked about sustainability in animal care, his first response is that it is unattainable, the Holy Grail, but that doesn't mean that you shouldn't try to get there. As he loves working in animal shelters and working for the common good, he keeps pursuing his vision of sustainability. When asked to define his version of sustainability in animal care, he said it is all about safety, taking care of people and animals, and protecting and expanding your mission to ensure growth is attainable. When asked about some of the biggest challenges for sustainability, he says that financial challenges in this time of economic uncertainty make it very hard to be successful, and further complicated by constant changes in priorities.

As an example in San Diego, his team set out to build a new cat adoption facility. By the time they got it done, the needs for cats in his region had plummeted, and the needs for dogs took off. As such they are now at 150-200% of capacity for dogs at their facilities.

On Pet Ministry

Some of the content in this book which you may not be expecting comes from the author's experience co-founding and growing a pet ministry. While the pet ministry he started was with Covenant Presbyterian Church in Charlotte, NC, readers of this book of any spiritual belief anywhere in the world can start their own local pet ministry achieving similar benefits as Alex and his colleagues did for their community's pets and people, and linking them all closer to their spiritual source while improving the sustainability of the area in many ways.

Here's how the author sees a pet ministry as being a foundational part of the relationship with local animal shelters and/or boarding facilities. Sustainability is all about something that is "lasting," and there is nothing more important than the souls of people and animals when the perspective is often about eternity.

Just to give four examples of how creating a pet ministry will benefit all types of pet businesses, here are four that the author's pet ministry has helped their community with in Charlotte, and can be done most places.

A Blessing of the Animal event from a Pet Ministry is typically one of the first and/or most popular pet ministry services. Strengthening the spiritual bond between animals and humans at these events is a great opportunity to expose more pet parents to more adoptable pets, and by improving pet mental health provides a larger pool of pets to be taken to pet training and pet boarding facilities.

Using canine therapy to help homeless neighbors brings some further purpose to the lives of giving people and pets, while also giving more homeless more opportunities to bond with pets that can help them turn their lives around. When pets are led to schools for students "on the spectrum," the presence of canine therapy further brings together these special students who otherwise may as not be as sociable, which can lead to long term benefits for the students, and by bringing them more into the mainstream provides more pet lovers to work or interact with animal shelters as well as all pet for profit businesses.

The same goes for mainstream people who attend universities, but who benefit from canine therapy during their stressful mid-term and final exam weeks every year.

Top 10 Learnings from Chapter 9 Meet the Experts

1. Sustainability Is Holistic: The 4 P's Matter (Pets, People, Planet, Profits)

This comprehensive framework encourages pet care professionals to think beyond singular issues like the environment and understand how animal welfare, staff well-being, environmental impact, and financial health are all interconnected. Applying this mindset improves strategic planning, aligns actions across departments, and results in longer-lasting, better-balanced outcomes.

2. Long-Term Thinking Is Essential

Sustainability in pet care must be focused on long-term solutions. As Jerrica Owen noted, sustainability means "long term," and Charlotte Biggs emphasized it is a "movement." This mindset helps businesses avoid quick fixes and instead invest in systems, facilities, and training that yield durable results, such as higher staff retention and lower operational costs.

3. Education Is the Cornerstone of Sustainable Success

Continuous education for staff and leaders is a recurring theme from nearly every expert in the chapter. Training improves implementation of SOPs, enhances animal care outcomes, and reduces costly errors. It also empowers staff, reducing burnout and turnover.

4.Standard Operating Procedures (SOPs) Drive Efficiency and Consistency

Many facilities lack effective SOPs, or their staff don't understand them. Educating staff on the "why" behind SOPs ensures buy-in and consistency. This results in more predictable processes, fewer mistakes, and better care outcomes.

5. Building and Design Decisions Have Long-Term Impacts

Experts like Scott Learned and Dianna Starr emphasize that poor design leads to higher long-term costs, health risks, and inefficiencies. Sustainable architecture and engineering—such as efficient layouts, durable materials, and smart drainage—can reduce energy usage, illness outbreaks, and cleaning costs.

6. Financial Planning and Profitability Enable Sustainability

Pet businesses, especially boarding and training facilities, must be profitable to invest in sustainability. Dom Hodgson's "premium pricing and niche positioning" strategy enables owners to fund improvements that support sustainability. Without margin, there's no mission.

7. Innovation and Early Adoption Create Competitive Advantage

Leaders like Jennifer Wolf-Pierson and Dan Poirier advocate trying new ideas and embracing innovation. This includes being early adopters of new products, practices, and technologies, which helps reduce costs and improve outcomes before competitors catch up.

8. Reduce Waste Through Smarter Operations

Jess Okon and Eve Molzhon show how simple shifts—like reducing paper towel usage or repurposing old building materials—can save money and the environment. These actions cut unnecessary spending and carbon footprints.

9. Staff Well-Being Is Critical to Operational Sustainability

Burnout, turnover, and understaffing are major threats. Solutions like enrichment programs, wellness support, and clearly communicated SOPs help retain talent. A happy, stable team leads to better animal care and smoother operations.

10. Community Engagement and Spiritual Connection Strengthen Purpose

The author's pet ministry work and Apryl Steele's socially conscious shelter philosophy highlight how engaging the community, spiritually or otherwise, creates stronger support systems. This leads to better fundraising, deeper volunteer pools, and a more resilient care ecosystem.

APPENDIX

Recommended Pet/Animal Care Resources and Organizations

Pet Care Consulting:
https://www.petbusinessmarketing.com/enrichu
https://thedoggurus.com/
https://phillipparisconsultants.com/
https://doghandleracademy.com/

Educational Associations: https://www.ibpsa.com/ , https://www.nacanet.org/ , https://www.petprofessionalguild.com/

Pet Care Software:
https://www.moego.pet/
https://www.gingrapp.com/

Staff Training:
https://packprotraining.com/

Pet Bedding:
https://kuranda.com/

Shelter Distributor:
https://sheltr-partners.org/

Environmental Sustainability:
https://petsustainability.org/

Recommended Books

Mindset The New Psychology of Success by Carol Dweck https://www.amazon.com/Mindset-Psychology-Carol-S-Dweck/dp/0345472322

Leading with Heart by John Baird and Edward Sullivan https://www.amazon.com/Leading-Heart-Conversations-Creativity-Purpose/dp/0063052938

Grit by Angela Duckworth https://www.amazon.com/Grit-Passion-Perseverance-Angela-Duckworth/dp/1501111108

Cultures of Growth by Mary C. Murphy https://www.amazon.com/Cultures-Growth-Transform-Individuals-Organizations/dp/1982172746

Diffusion of Innovations by Everett Rogers https://www.amazon.com/Diffusion-Innovations-5th-Everett-Rogers/dp/0743222091

The Catalyst How to Change Anyone's Mind by Jonah Berger https://www.amazon.com/Diffusion-Innovations-5th-Everett-Rogers/dp/0743222091

Positioning by Al Ries and Jack Trout https://www.amazon.com/Diffusion-Innovations-5th-Everett-Rogers/dp/0743222091

The Story Factor by Annette Simmons https://www.amazon.com/Diffusion-Innovations-5th-Everett-Rogers/dp/0743222091

**Kellogg on Branding in a Hyperconnected World
By Alice Tybout and Tim Calkins**
https://www.amazon.com/Diffusion-Innovations-5th-Everett-Rogers/dp/0743222091

Made to Stick by Chip Heath and Dan Heath
https://www.amazon.com/Diffusion-Innovations-5th-Everett-Rogers/dp/0743222091

The Power of Moments by Chip Heath and Dan Heath https://www.amazon.com/Diffusion-Innovations-5th-Everett-Rogers/dp/0743222091

Designing Your Life by Bill Burnett and Dale Evans https://www.amazon.com/Designing-Your-Life-Well-Lived-Joyful/dp/1101875321

Sustainability Educational Materials by Kinn Kleanbowl - www.kinninc.com

Time Studies – Videos and Educational Materials
https://kinninc.com/time-studies/

Client Success Story Testimonials Video Series
https://kinninc.com/pet-services/video-series/

Pet Services educational materials
https://kinninc.com/pet-services/

Animal Shelters educational materials
https://kinninc.com/animal-shelters/

Advantages of true bowl cleanliness
https://kinninc.com/kleanbowl-challenge-2/

Commercial Dishwasher Research
https://kinninc.com/wp-content/uploads/2021/03/Kinn_Dishwasher_Research.pdf

Environmental Life Cycle Analysis
https://kinninc.com/wp-content/uploads/2021/03/04_PSC_Kinn_Case_Study.pdf

Kleanbowl Time and Cost Savings Estimator
https://kinninc.com/resources/kleanbowl-estimator/

Staff Training Video
http://KleanbowlStaffTraining.com

Staff Engagement & Retention Benefits
http://ilovepetcare.com

------- End

www.ingramcontent.com/pod-product-compliance
Lightning Source LLC
Chambersburg PA
CBHW051426090426
42737CB00014B/2848